Data Quality ROI

A Playbook for
Business-Driven Data Quality

Gaurav Patole

Technics Publications
SEDONA, ARIZONA

TECHNICS PUBLICATIONS

115 Linda Vista, Sedona, AZ 86336 USA
https://www.TechnicsPub.com

Edited by Steve Hoberman
Cover design by Lorena Molinari

First Printing 2025

Copyright © 2025 by Gaurav Patole

ISBN, print ed.   9798898160197
ISBN, Kindle ed.   9798898160203
ISBN, PDF ed.   9798898160210

Endorsements

How many times have you heard "We don't just care about Data Quality"? As a Chief Data Officer in a global semiconductor company, I've seen firsthand how poor data quality can derail transformation efforts, even more in the AI era we are in now. This book delivers a rare combination of deep expertise and practical frameworks that any organization— regardless of maturity—can use to take control of its data, to adopt a Fit-for-Purpose mindset focused exclusively on the data that drives decisions, revenue, and risk mitigation. Whether you're leading a data initiative or starting to build a data culture, this is the go-to guide.

Patrick Attallah, Chief Data Officer at NXP Semiconductors

The core idea in this book—that data quality is fundamentally a communication challenge—is a powerful one. It provides a useful framework for data teams who are struggling to translate their efforts into a language that resonates with business stakeholders and fosters a culture of shared data accountability.

Dr. Sebastian Wernicke, Bestselling Author of 'Data Inspired', Partner- Oxera Consulting

There are many books written about data governance, but most of them focus on the how (like the famous DMBOK). As a result, data governance gets a reputation for being something you do to avoid fines or other government-forced compliance. Gaurav Patole has done something unique – rather than focusing on how to do data governance, he actually tells a story explaining why it is important. And as a bonus, he ties it into Sir Isaac Newton and his famous laws. For anyone who builds data pipelines, creates data governance, or even if you simply use data (which should be everyone, right?) I highly recommend this book.

Jeff Nieman, Fortune 100 Global Data, AI & Analytics Leader, Senior Director of Data Strategy and Visualisation at BestBuy

It is with great pride and pleasure that I am recommending this book. Gaurav and I worked together some years back and our work was focused on Data Quality. One of the biggest challenges we faced was bringing the value of the work we were doing to life and getting our stakeholders to not only pay attention but also to look at the data they were using and treat it as the asset it is. This book is the culmination of those learnings and Gaurav's journey along the way. What I love most is how pragmatic and practical it is. It is not a book teaching you how to DO data quality. There are many of those. This book gets to the heart of changing your stakeholder's mindset. It is a must read to give you great advice, backed by knowledge and "been there, done that" experience.

Sue Geuens, Director Data Governance & Product Data at Elsevier

I am very pleased to see this book becoming a reality. Gaurav brings a fresh perspective on the topic of Data Quality and makes an interesting bridge between business and IT when it comes to the communication and implementation process. We have shared some interesting experiences in Thoughtworks, working for several clients on complex Data Engineering and Data Governance initiatives. Regardless of the architectural choices and existing tooling, the common pain point was always related to Data Quality. Everyone agrees that ownership is key, but most organizations lack a concrete and pragmatic approach on how to address the issue. Gaurav has been genuinely concerned about making people care about Data Quality in the first place and making sure ownership is an integral part of the process. I highly recommend this book for everyone involved in large scale data initiatives.

Alexandre Goedert, VP of Engineering, SurePay

Poor data quality is often the hidden root cause behind stalled transformations and underperforming programs. Yet, many business leaders still struggle to address it proactively, held back by a lack of data literacy and unclear accountability. Drawing on years of hands-on experience, Gaurav has written a remarkable playbook that bridges the gap between the urgency of data quality and the will to act. It is a valuable step-guide for data leaders, helping them connect data quality to the business outcomes that matter most.

Hector Bernal, Global Data Leader

Having worked alongside Gaurav through some of the most demanding data transformation programs, I've seen his brilliance in action, leading and delivering enterprise-scale data governance and quality initiatives with a level of impact that's truly unprecedented. This book reflects that same rare mix of vision, depth, and execution. Gaurav doesn't just explain data quality, he humanizes it, repositions it, and makes it impossible to ignore. For any data or business leader seeking clarity, alignment, and trust in their decisions, this book is a masterstroke.

Subeer Sehgal, Head, AI & Data Governance Strategy at Fractal

More and more people talk about data and data quality these days — because it matters. It drives AI, shapes business decisions, and changes how we work. But those conversations often get too technical, too quickly. Or they drift into an ocean of buzzwords. This book takes a refreshing turn. It uses Newton's laws to explain data in a fun, unusual way. It's clear, surprising, and full of ideas that will spark your curiosity.

Aleksejs Plotnikovs,
Author of 'Data Management Strategy at Microsoft', Founder of chief data.ai

A practical, compelling guide to transforming data quality from a technical task into a strategic business process.

Dr. Tejasvi Addagada, SVP & Head - AI & GenAI Governance, HDFC Bank Limited

Data quality is the foundation upon which the success of AI and business intelligence is built." In today's AI-driven world, Gaurav's book, "Data Quality ROI: A Playbook for business-driven data quality," is a timely exploration of this critical subject. I wholeheartedly endorse this work, as it offers a unique perspective on how data quality can be communicated effectively as a business narrative. Gaurav's incorporation of a Newtonian approach adds depth and clarity, making complex concepts accessible to all. This book is a valuable resource for any organization seeking to enhance its data processes and for individuals who wish to gain a deeper understanding of data quality to leverage the power of accurate data for strategic advancement.

Kaustubh Khatkhdekar, Friend and Data Quality Advisor at ABN AMRO Bank Netherlands

Gaurav's ingenious Newtonian approach to demystify data quality by addressing the "laws of data quality" is both brilliant and refreshingly practical - transforming abstract concepts into actionable insights that stick. His brutally honest take on why DQ programs fail, coupled with real-world examples that hit uncomfortably close to home, makes this book a wake-up call for every organization struggling with data trust. Having collaborated with Gaurav, I can attest that his passion for making data quality accessible and human-centered shines through every page. This is a must-read for anyone who manages, cares about, or has ever complained about data quality - which, let's face it, is all of us!

Tiankai Feng, Friend, colleague, and bestselling author of "Humanizing Data Strategy"

Rarely do you find a book which is as relevant for a new associate as it is for the CDO. This book presents a refreshing take on data quality which is comprehensive as well as simple to grasp. Gaurav's wide range of experience in varied industries from defining strategy to managing data operations, has helped him craft a data quality framework which aptly blends fundamental quality principles with practical implementation guidance. If you could read only one book to understand how data quality needs to be addressed at an organizational level, I believe this should be one to help you drive data excellence in your organization.

Dwaipayan Das, Mentor and Global Head, Infosys Data Governance Practice

To everyone who believed in me.

Acknowledgments

It's finally happening, and honestly, even as I write these words, it still feels unreal to say it out loud: I am an author. There were many moments throughout this journey when I wasn't sure I could truly pull it off.

And, yes, the book absolutely *had* to be about data quality. After more than a decade working in this space, I remain endlessly fascinated by its complexities and deeply passionate about making it better and more accessible for everyone. Yet, this isn't *my* book alone. Every idea, challenge, and insight within these pages owes itself to the generosity, wisdom, and passion of many people.

Getting here was certainly not a stroke of luck; it was built on the unwavering support and sacrifices of many. My deepest gratitude goes to my grandparents, who lovingly raised me and instilled the values of perseverance and simplicity. To my father and my sister, who always believed in my potential and encouraged me to chase meaningful pursuits, thank you for your unwavering faith. To my mother, I know I have your blessings from heaven.

And to my incredible wife, Ashwini, and my wonderful son, Sriyansh, I could have never made it this far without your boundless patience and support. You graciously allowed me to dedicate countless late nights and weekends to this project, and for that, I am eternally grateful. This milestone is as much yours as it is mine.

To my colleagues and clients: our countless conversations have shaped every chapter. You challenged assumptions, shared real-world struggles, and celebrated hard-won wins. Your voices echo throughout this book, reminding me that data quality is, at its core, a human endeavor.

A heartfelt thank you to all the esteemed endorsers of this book: Karthik Ravindran, Hector Bernal, Jeff Nieman, Dr. Sebastian Wernicke, Patrick Attallah, Dwaipayan Das, Subeer Sehgal, Kaustubh Khatkhedkar, Aleksejs Plotnikovs, Alexandre Goedert, Dr.Tejasvi Addagada, Sue Geuens, and Tiankai Feng. Your knowledge, wisdom, and leadership continue to inspire me every single day. Your willingness to support this project means the world.

A special thank you to Steve Hoberman for believing in this work and giving me the opportunity to publish. Your guidance turned a long-held dream into reality.

Finally, to the broader data management community, thank you for your curiosity, your questions, and your relentless drive to improve. It is your collective energy that makes this field so rewarding, and this book wouldn't exist without your support.

Contents

Foreword

Data quality is amongst the most acknowledged and yet the most debated topics of our time. In the current age of AI that we are traversing, "AI being only as good as the data that it uses" and good data anchoring on the quality of data, is generally well understood. Yet in practice, the why, the what, the who, and the how of practices to create and maintain quality data are debated intensely with diverse opinions and a lack of general alignment. The differences stem from data quality generally being viewed as a "technical" accountability and a subject of debate on the technical solutions for it. While technology has an essential role to play in enabling and scaling data quality, technology in and by itself is not the solution for data quality.

Data quality is a team sport. It is an organizational and cross-functional team sport, anchored on the purpose of each organization and its people who serve the purpose. The purpose of an organization shapes its business, whether for-profit or not-for-profit. Every business generates, acquires, and uses data to shape its growth. In the age of AI, data is used by AI models, agents, and applications for training, reasoning, and inference. The effectiveness of AI can only be as impactful as the quality of the data used by and for each AI use case.

This fundamental also holds true for other and prior data use cases. The quality of data has facets that are shared across use cases and facets that are contextual to each use case. The contexts and considerations that shape the facets are organization-wide, needing cross-functional teams and people to partake in the lifecycle of data, contributing to the shaping and quality of data for its use cases. A team sport mindset and play are needed to practice the virtues of data quality and realize its applied value. Business functions in an organization, specifically, lead an organization's applied contexts and have a substantial role of leadership to play in shaping and scaling an organization's data quality investments.

When I learnt that Gaurav is writing a book on data quality, I knew instinctively that it would be different, in a great way. Reading the book validated my instinct. Gaurav is a seasoned data practitioner who has dedicated his career to the practice of data and helping global organizations navigate their data journeys. I have learned a lot from him from our conversations on our lived data journeys and from his shorter form content. With this book, Gaurav has addressed a long-standing gap in the literature on data quality. He has synthesized the essence of data quality in the form that it is meant to be explained and understood, as a business narrative accessible to cross-functional leaders and practitioners.

The principles and concepts introduced in this book, when practiced, can help you achieve transformative outcomes with your data. Having led multiple such journeys, both within the organization I serve and with our customers, I could see many of my lived experiences playing out as a movie as I read each chapter. I was also able to gather several golden nuggets of wisdom, often overlooked, captured here in simple and relatable constructs.

This is a book that is meant to be read chapter by chapter. Each chapter builds incrementally in accruing a treasure trove of learnings. The flow from debunking the myths of data quality, to laying out its foundations, followed by a unique approach in applying the concepts of Newton's laws of motion to unpack the essence, to practical organizational guidance including the opportunities for and with AI, culminating with guiding principles for technology solutions to scale the practice, covers an end-to-end spectrum in helping readers form a vantage view of data quality that integrates the why, the what, the who, and the how.

This book that you hold in your hands is a work of leadership that will create clarity and generate energy for data quality as an organization-wide team sport. It is a book to be read and practiced by business and technology leaders and teams. I hope you enjoy it and learn as much from it as I did.

I am grateful for the opportunity to write this foreword for this incredible work of passion by Gaurav.

Karthik Ravindran

General Manager, Worldwide Data Platforms GTM

Microsoft Corporation

Why this Book?

First things first—this is *not* another book on *"how"* to do data quality. There are already plenty of great technical books and resources available on this topic in the market. I don't want to add just another book to that pile.

Instead, this book focuses on something that's often overlooked: the *"why"* and *"who"* of data quality.

More specifically, it's about 'business' and 'communication,' on how we can engage business stakeholders, drive ownership, and make them care about data quality in a way that resonates with them.

There is a reason why I started writing this book. Data quality isn't a new topic. It has been written about, debated, and invested in for decades. And yet, despite all that attention, most organizations continue to struggle with it.

Poor data still delays digital transformation, penalizes organizations, confuses decision-makers, and erodes trust in even the most well-designed reports and dashboards.

Over the past decade, I have been fortunate to work across multiple organizations, industries, and cultures in the data management space, and when it came to data quality, I kept encountering a common frustration:

"Our business doesn't care about data quality. They don't own it, they don't understand it, and they don't control it."

Variations of this same sentiment can be seen across industry conferences, LinkedIn posts, and hallway conversations between data professionals:

"Why is data quality always the responsibility of IT?"
"My business knows they should own data quality, but they just don't step up!"
"IT can't fix data if they don't even know what it means—this is a business problem!"

To be fair, these are all valid concerns. The logic seems simple enough—business teams know the data best, so they should be accountable for its quality. Yet, despite how straightforward this sounds, business stakeholders often hesitate to take ownership. Data quality has mostly been just a technical challenge. And it continues to be treated as a back-office, IT-driven initiative; often disconnected from the people who know the data best.

The stakes are even higher now

The stakes are even higher now, thanks to multi-billion-dollar AI initiatives across organizations. Today, AI and automation have transitioned from pilot projects to the core of corporate strategy, and with this shift comes unprecedented risk.

Poor data quality no longer skews monthly reports; it can weaponize bias, undermine predictive models, and cascade costly errors across automated processes. If your organization truly intends to build AI and advanced analytics into its core operations, it cannot afford to relegate data quality to a back-burner concern. Models trained on incomplete, inaccurate, or biased data will someday lead to wrong predictions, lost opportunities, and wasted investment.

As W. Edwards Deming once said:

> *"If you can't describe what you are doing as a process, you don't know what you're doing."*

And I'd add, if you don't understand how your data is created, shared, governed, and trusted, your AI ambitions will remain just that: ambitions.

The urgency is real. And the need for a clear, shared understanding has never been greater. —which is exactly why I've called this book Data Quality ROI: A Playbook for Business-Driven Data Quality." Because at its core, it's about shifting the conversation from just fixing bad data to understanding the return on treating data quality as a business priority.

My personal journey with simplicity

If there's one thing that has defined how I look at problems, especially complex ones like data quality, it's simplicity.

That instinct didn't come from books or courses. It came from my childhood.

I was raised by my grandparents in very modest financial circumstances. We had limited means, and I grew up with a deep awareness of how fragile our safety net was. My sister and I were taught to be cautious; to think carefully before taking risks. If something didn't work out, we didn't have a backup net to fall onto.

Naturally, I had to keep my choices simple. I didn't chase elite schools or shiny opportunities. I believed that if I could think clearly and make a difference through my work, I'd find my place regardless of credentials or pedigree.

That belief shaped how I worked. Throughout my career, I broke down problems until they made sense; until they were manageable, solvable, and relatable to the people I was working with. I didn't look for grand solutions. I looked for understandable ones.

This book is no different.

I've tried to bring that same lens to data quality; not as an academician or a consultant, but as a practitioner who believes in clarity over complexity.

Why bring Newton into all this?

When I decided to dig deeper into the disconnect between data quality efforts and business engagement, I began having more focused conversations. I spoke with business stakeholders across different clients, industry experts, and my extensive data network on LinkedIn. What I curated was a series of fascinating insights and stories about why this disconnect exists and how business genuinely perceives data quality. My goal was to make these insights clear, accessible, and easy to understand for everyone in the industry. But, I wasn't entirely sure how to best articulate such a complex, often abstract, set of observations.

At the same time, I happened to be reading about Sir Isaac Newton and his work. What struck me wasn't just the brilliance of his discoveries, but the elegance with which he explained them. Newton didn't just study the laws of motion, he framed them in a way that made the invisible visible. He helped the world understand how things moved, through simple, universal laws. His approach to explaining the complex concepts of our physical world through three fundamental laws of motion was brilliant.

And I tried to replicate the same approach for data quality. What if we could describe how data flows, interacts, and sometimes breaks inside organizations, using simple, universal "laws" that would make sense to both business and technical teams?

Just as Newton's laws explain how motion works in the physical world, I realized I could define a set of "laws" to explain how data quality works in the business world. Hence the Newtonian Approach!

What you'll learn from this book

This book reflects stories, frustrations, insights, and breakthroughs I've collected over the years.

It's not a guide to implementing data quality. It's a guide to thinking differently about how we solve the data quality problem—together!

By the end of this book, you will:

- Understand the real reasons why data quality fails in most organizations.

- Learn how business perception and language shape data ownership.

- Explore four simple, yet powerful "laws" that govern how data quality behaves inside organizations.

- See practical strategies for shifting mindsets, building support, and moving from friction to shared accountability.

Whether you're a Chief Data Officer, a data governance lead, a data quality SME, a business stakeholder, an IT lead, or a data analyst caught in the middle of data quality chaos, I hope this book gives you not just insight, but clarity. And above all, I hope it helps you frame data quality not just as an operational necessity, but as a strategic business asset—one that deserves real attention, real investment, and real return.

At the heart of every data problem lies a human conversation waiting to happen.
And conversations, when done right, can move mountains.

ONE

Data Quality Beliefs

One of the often-overlooked reasons why data quality programs struggle or even fail isn't a lack of data quality expertise, technology, or good intentions. In fact, there's plenty of strong DQ literature available in the market. The problem lies in starting with the wrong foundation. One of the reasons DQ programs often fail is that organizations have read or done the right things in the wrong order. They initially absorbed a set of false or weakly true things, and those formed the foundation of their DQ worldview. As a result, every new decision, strategy, or tool is built upon assumptions that were never accurate to begin with.

That's why foundational clarity is so critical. When it comes to data management in general, make sure your foundations are high quality and clear. The best way to establish a high-quality foundation is to read and comprehend original data management literature, such as the DAMA-DMBOK. That is some serious foundational knowledge curated by experts in this field.

When you begin with a strong, well-informed foundation, everything else—new tools, evolving concepts, and practical applications—can be understood and re-derived with confidence. You're no longer reacting blindly to trends; you're making deliberate, informed choices that align with your organization's unique goals.

Breaking common data quality misconceptions

My discussions around this topic with business and tech leaders have surfaced some of the most common beliefs about data quality that keep showing up in organizations across industries, teams, and even leadership levels. These beliefs may seem harmless on the surface, but they often become the reason why data quality efforts don't deliver results.

Before we define what data quality means, it's essential to clarify what it *doesn't* mean. Before we discuss engaging business stakeholders or shifting organizational mindsets, we need to first *unlearn* what doesn't serve us. I've shared below some of the most common claims I've encountered and heard, and I have tried to be a bit creative here. Hopefully, it will resonate.

In the section below, *"they"* refers to the general perception, common wisdom, or shared assumptions floating around in the organization or industry. It's not pointing fingers at a person or team, but rather calling out those default beliefs that people absorb over time without questioning.

Think of "they" as:

- Legacy mindsets in organizations
- Outdated consulting slides
- Casual advice passed around at conferences
- Team leads or execs who are well-meaning but misinformed
- Buzzwords from vendors
- Hallway hearsay

So, in effect, "they" is everyone and no one. It's the collective voice of assumptions, traditions, and shortcuts we've often normalized in our day-to-day data work.

I have followed these beliefs with the following *"But ask yourself"* statements, which allows you to pause, step back, intentionally think, and challenge these assumptions using logic, context, and your own experience. These prompts are simplified to help you build a stronger foundation for engaging business stakeholders in meaningful data quality conversations. The aim isn't to argue, but to invite perspective. Each organization may interpret these slightly differently, but the goal is the same: to start with the right mindset!

#1: "They say..."

"Data quality can be achieved 100%."

But ask yourself…

Is it really possible to clean every piece of data across your entire organization—especially with so many systems, sources, formats, and an ever-growing volume of information? Even if it were possible, is that level of perfection really necessary?

Chasing 100% data quality across every dataset within your data estate is like trying to boil the ocean. It drains time, energy, and budget without offering a proportionate return on value. Instead, isn't a smarter approach to focus on "data that matters"? It's about ensuring that the data is accurate, complete, and trusted for the specific use cases or data sources that matter most to the business. That's where concepts like identifying critical data elements come in.

Not all data deserves equal attention. Data quality is not "all or nothing." It exists on a spectrum. Perfection is a trap; relevance is the real goal.

#2: "They say…"

"Data quality is a one-time cleansing activity."

But ask yourself…

If you clean your data today, will it stay clean tomorrow? Are you sure errors, inconsistencies, and duplicates won't just creep back in? If bad data keeps coming in, won't you keep cleaning it forever?

Data Cleansing is only part of the equation. Without fixing the root cause of data issues—whether it's broken business processes, source system configurations, unclear definitions, or DQ rules that avoid human error—you're just sweeping the floor while the roof's leaking.

#3: "They say..."

"Data quality projects are complex, expensive, and take too long."

But ask yourself...

Is complexity really the problem, or is it unclear goals and roles?

I'm personally not fond of calling data quality a complex task. Because, to be honest, it isn't if you break it into understandable pieces.

Many DQ efforts can feel overwhelming because there is no consensus on what "done" looks like. Is the goal to clean a dataset? Monitor a data pipeline? Set up a dashboard? Improve a business process? When that clarity is missing, things spiral into endless tasks.

Wouldn't it help to start small, pick one use case that matters, and show one win? It's important to keep it grounded. When people see progress, momentum builds and complexity starts to fade. It's critical to understand that DQ is an iterative process and needs to be gradually scaled up with the right resourcing strategy. Also, don't start with address standardization from day one; otherwise, you will regret your job!

#4: "They say..."

"Data quality and data validation are the same thing."

But ask yourself...

Is checking for missing values the same as ensuring your data makes sense?

Validation is just the tip of the iceberg. Yes, it's useful to check if dates are in the right format or if all fields are filled, but that doesn't mean your data is correct, consistent, or meaningful.

Real data quality goes deeper. Are we tracking the right things? Is this data useful for decisions? Do people trust it? That's more than just ticking off validation rules.

#5: "They say..."

"Data quality is IT's responsibility."

But ask yourself...

Can IT improve the quality of something it doesn't fully understand?

IT teams manage systems, pipelines, and tools, but they don't always understand the business meaning behind the data. If a customer's status field is wrong, IT can't tell if it should be "active" or "inactive" unless someone from the business tells them what those statuses actually mean. Business teams know the *why* behind the data, and without that, IT can only guess.

Data quality is a shared job—business provides the context, IT provides the structure. Even your data teams cannot handle data quality alone unless you have specific data domain experts sitting in the business teams.

#6: "They say..."

"If we establish data governance, we'll automatically improve data quality."

But ask yourself...

Can rules and policies alone fix bad data, broken habits, and unclear responsibilities?

It's often assumed that the data governance team will also take care of data quality. The data governance role is essential, no doubt, but it's only a starting point. You can define roles, create DQ policies, and assign stewards, but nothing changes unless people understand their role in improving data.

It's also worth noting that governance and quality don't always share the same business pain points or use cases.

Improving data quality requires action, not just oversight. That requires a dedicated team or at least a sub-function within the governance setup focused specifically on data quality. Their job is to primarily translate governance into real change through:

- Hands-on support and enablement for data quality checks
- Collaboration between IT and business to solve business issues
- Support for root cause analysis and remediation of issues
- Ownership of the day-to-day mechanics (implementation) of DQ.

Governance gives structure. But quality comes from consistent execution, shared accountability, and cross-functional collaboration. Policy alone won't clean your data—people will!

Data governance gives structure to the overall DQ program, but action gives results. That action on data stems from mutual collaboration across teams, consistent follow-through, and not just policy documents.

#7: "They say…"

"Let's outsource data quality to an external team and let them handle it completely."

But ask yourself…

Can someone outside your business really fix what they don't live and breathe every day?

Often, organizations outsource their data quality efforts to external consultancy or IT firms.

External consultants can help set up processes, frameworks, and tools—but they can't magically understand your business logic, your unique workflows, or your customer expectations. They weren't there when the data was created, and they won't be there when decisions are made.

You can bring in help, use their expertise and borrow their frameworks and templates, but you can't outsource responsibility. Business teams still need to engage, validate, and own their part. Without their fingerprints on the process, you end up with "clean" data that's technically correct but might be practically useless. Data quality isn't a side task—it's a team sport.

#8: "They say…"

"Data quality issues should only be fixed at the source."

But ask yourself...

Is it realistic—or even fair—to expect source teams to fix every downstream problem?

Source systems are often designed for operational speed, rather than analytical precision. The people managing those systems aren't always aware of how the data will be used later, or where it ends up. And let's be honest, no team sets out to create bad data.

In reality, data passes through many hands and systems before it's consumed. Each step adds complexity, context, and risk. Instead of pointing fingers at the source, it's far more productive to ask: Where in the journey can we collaborate to prevent and resolve issues together?

Clean data is everyone's job. Ownership must flow across teams and not get stuck at the origin.

#9: "They say..."

"Let's buy a DQ tool and we're done!"

But ask yourself...

Is a tool really the answer without the right people, processes, and understanding behind it?

Tools can help *automate* checks, identify issues, and sometimes even suggest fixes, but they don't define what good data means for your business. They don't resolve ownership issues, close communication gaps, or fix broken processes.

Buying a DQ tool without a broader strategy is like purchasing gym equipment and hoping to get fit without ever exercising. The real transformation comes from how you enable the tool for your audience—not just that you have one.

#10: "They say..."

"Buy any DQ tool, all tools do the same things."

But ask yourself...

If all tools were the same, why do so many vendors exist in the industry and so many organizations still struggle to get results after implementation?

Not all data quality tools cover end-to-end DQ management. Some excel at profiling but lack robust cleansing or standardization features. Others may support rule creation but offer no real remediation workflows. Some tools may look great in demos but fall short in terms of integration, scalability, or cross-functional usability.

Tool selection should be led by business needs, not vendor promises. And it's not just about features—it's about fit. How well does the tool support your team, tech stack, governance model, and long-term roadmap?

Choosing the right DQ or DG platform is a comprehensive process in itself. We'll get into that in later chapters. Don't buy the hype; buy what works for you.

Two

Foundations of Data Quality

Before we dive into the specifics of business-driven data quality in the upcoming chapters, it's crucial to establish some foundational concepts. This chapter may be a repetition of what's already available in standard books and materials on data quality. But it will also reflect on what I've learned through real-world DQ projects, frustrations, Zoom debates, and those "a-ha" moments that come only after seeing things break and then fixing them.

These are not textbook definitions. They are practical pointers meant to help you connect the dots as we move deeper into the specifics of business-driven data quality.

What is data quality?

Let's begin with the obvious but often misunderstood question: *What does data quality really mean?*

Here is my definition of data quality:

Data quality is the degree to which data is accurate, usable, trusted, relevant, and fit for purpose—delivered in a way that meets the specific needs of the consumers.

That last part is key: *meets the specific needs of the consumers.* Because at the heart of it, data quality isn't about perfection—it's about usefulness.

You don't need perfect data. You need purposeful data.

It's about ensuring that the right people get the right data, at the right time, in the right form, to make the right decisions. Data that's timely and trusted enough to act on.

This definition reminds us that data quality is not just a checklist. I know it's cliché, but it's true. It's not just about fixing typos or removing duplicates. It's about understanding what the business needs from data and making sure the data can reliably deliver on those needs.

That's why, throughout this book, we'll keep coming back to the same idea: engage the business. Because data quality isn't just a technical standard to be maintained by IT; it is, first and foremost, a powerful business enabler. And when the business clearly sees this and initiates action, everything starts to change.

Types of data quality checks

One of the primary reasons data quality is often miscategorized as purely an IT or operational function comes from a common misconception: that it's solely a collection of technical validation checks applied across data pipelines. While these checks are undeniably critical, they represent just one facet of the much larger data quality landscape.

Fundamentally, there are two broad categories of data quality checks, **technical data quality checks** and **business data quality checks**, and they serve very different purposes:

Technical data quality checks are the most common checks applied directly to the 'data' itself, ensuring its structural integrity and adherence to basic rules. Technical data quality checks are typically automated validations that data engineers and developers apply at various stages: during data ingestion, transformation, or when data is curated for specific uses. It ensures the plumbing is working correctly. These are also often referred to as data validations, engineering tests, or IT checks. Questions to answer include:

- Are all mandatory fields populated?
- Are date formats consistent?
- Has the table been refreshed according to its SLA?
- Is the row count matching between source and target?
- Are foreign keys aligned across joins?

These checks are essential, but they operate in a vacuum and don't necessarily validate the business logic.

In many organizations, this becomes the entire data quality conversation—developers or analysts checking against rules, pipeline teams raising alerts, and source system teams being blamed. And when that loop fails to fix things, business stakeholders are finally pulled in to "resolve" something they were never involved in defining.

Let me try to illustrate this with a story.

A few years ago, while working with a major consulting firm, our team was responsible for preparing weekly sales reports for the CFO and COO. It was Christmas week, and all our reports passed every technical DQ rule—no missing values, pipeline ran on time, validations succeeded. So, we sent leadership the dashboard. The next morning, we got a furious call. According to the report, **$1 billion in sales** had been generated in the Middle East region in a single week. It was a staggering number considering the region had never even crossed that mark *annually*, let alone during the slowest sales week of the year.

It turns out that a single record had a mis-entered sales value, which inflated the total. The business user who spot-checks the final numbers before distribution was on holiday. The report passed every technical rule but failed the reality test.

No doubt, technical validation checks are essential, but they operate in a vacuum. They don't validate whether the numbers make sense to the business—just whether they passed a rule. Remember, IT can only guarantee data availability, not data accuracy.

If technical checks ensure that data flows correctly through pipelines, business checks ensure the data actually makes "sense" in the real world. Nobody understands that real-world context better than the functional teams who use the data daily. Sales knows what sales volumes are reasonable. Finance knows what a valid invoice looks like. The supply chain knows which SKUs should be in which warehouse. In some organizations, these checks are also referred to as Functional Data Checks.

That's why business data quality checks are not about validating structure or format—they're about validating meaning.

These checks are grounded in business logic, domain knowledge, expected outcomes, and human judgment. Questions to answer include:

- Do these sales figures make sense for this region?

- Is the apparent sales performance decline simply because of seasonal variance within a business, or a structural drop?

- Is a predictive model's input distribution drifting (e.g., customer behavior, transaction features) in a way that will degrade forecasts or recommendations?

- Are missed SLAs caused by data pipeline errors or bad CRM entries — and are those delays costing us revenue or customers?

Unlike technical validations, these aren't always obvious or easy to codify. Often, they're implicit; held in someone's intuition, not in documentation. That's why it's critical to extract this context before development begins on any data product, report, or pipeline.

Let's go back to the example from earlier: the $1 billion in phantom sales during Christmas week.

Technically, everything passed. The fields were filled, the formats were correct, and the pipeline was refreshed. But business-wise, it was nonsense. No one had ever seen such numbers from that region—not even annually. The only reason this error slipped through was that there were no business checks in place to say, "This number is unrealistic."

That's the danger of relying solely on technical rules: you can pass every check and still be wrong.

Creating effective business checks requires a collaborative, iterative process between data teams and functional stakeholders. It's part education, part exploration. And it doesn't happen overnight.

We'll cover how to drive this alignment in later chapters. But for now, let's remember:

If technical checks ensure the pipes are clean, business checks ensure the water is drinkable.

Both are essential!

Below is a quick tabular summary for easy reference.

Aspect	Technical DQ Checks	Business DQ Checks
Focus Area	Data structure, format, completeness	Business logic, process alignment, contextual accuracy
Ownership	Data engineers, developers	Domain owners, functional leads
Examples	Null checks, Format validation, Record counts, SLA freshness checks	"Does this sales number make sense?" "Do invoice totals really match expectations?" "Are product quantities realistic?"
Primary Objective	Ensure data is technically valid and flows correctly	Ensure data makes sense for decision-making
When Applied	During ingestion, transformation, or data movement	Captured during requirement analysis, implemented during ingestion, transformation, or data movement
Common Tools Used	Data pipeline validation tools, data platform internal checkers, ETL monitoring tools	Data quality tools, data profiling tools, or custom code logic
Blind Spots	Doesn't detect logical errors in content	Harder to standardize, depends on business engagement

Data quality-related terminologies:

The entire data quality spectrum often comes with its own specialized vocabulary, and it's easy to get lost with similar acronyms and overlapping concepts. To truly understand our topic of business-driven data quality, it's helpful to demystify some of these frequently encountered terms. While each has its own nuances, all of them intersect with data quality in meaningful ways.

Data observability

Often falls into the category of technical DQ checks, data observability is like a sophisticated, real-time diagnostic system for your data ecosystem. It involves continuously monitoring the health, freshness, volume, distribution, drifts, and schema of your data, as well as the performance of the pipelines that move it. Data observability is a growing domain, and many specialized vendors are making it more automated and attractive, thanks to AI agents.

Data contracts

Just as any good business relationship relies on clear agreements, effective data quality depends on formalizing expectations between those who create data and those who use it. This is where data contracts come in. Think of them as a set of service-level agreements (SLAs) or explicit blueprints that define the structure, format, semantics, quality expectations, and timeliness of data being exchanged.

Data contracts are the backbone of the entire "Shift Left" phenomenon that you might have heard about in conferences or read on LinkedIn. It essentially means shifting your data quality left—meaning to embed quality expectations at the point of data production. By establishing these upfront agreements, data producers commit to delivering data that meets specific standards, and data consumers know precisely what to expect. This significantly reduces misunderstandings, prevents breaking changes in data pipelines, and ensures that data delivered is truly fit for purpose, thereby building inherent trust and reliability into your data flows.

DQ testing versus DQ monitoring versus data cleansing: distinct stages of quality assurance

These three terms are often used interchangeably, but they represent distinct, albeit complementary, activities in the data quality journey:

- **DQ testing:** This is a point-in-time validation. It involves executing specific rules or benchmarks to confirm data quality at a particular moment. You may perform DQ testing after implementing a new system, conducting a significant data migration, or making a major change to an ETL pipeline. It's like a quality

assurance check for a specific release or project
milestone.

- **DQ monitoring:** In contrast to testing, DQ Monitoring
  is about ongoing and continuous tracking of data quality
  metrics over time. This involves setting up automated
  processes to regularly check for items such as missing
  values, duplicates, data drift (unexpected changes in data
  patterns), and adherence to established rules. For
  example, a dashboard displays daily counts of failed
  records, alerting the data team if nulls exceed 2% or if the
  record volume suddenly drops by 50%. It's the daily,
  weekly, or even hourly health check of your data, alerting
  you to issues as they emerge.

- **Data cleansing:** Cleansing is mostly an after-effect,
  which is the remediation process itself. It refers to the
  actual act of identifying and correcting errors,
  inconsistencies, and inaccuracies within your data. It's
  the tangible work of fixing *bad* data. This could involve
  correcting misspelled names, updating outdated
  addresses, removing duplicate customer records, or
  filling in truly missing mandatory values. Data cleansing
  is typically triggered by issues identified through testing
  or monitoring to restore data to an acceptable quality
  state.

Data standardization versus data enrichment versus data harmonization

These three concepts often work hand-in-hand to transform data, making it more usable, valuable, and unified. While they can sometimes be part of a larger **cleansing project**, their primary focus is on improving the structure, completeness, or interoperability of data, often even if the original data wasn't strictly "erroneous" but simply inconsistent or lacking context. Their common goal is to enhance the overall utility and interconnectedness of data:

- **Data standardization**: It refers to converting data into a common format, structure, or representation so that downstream systems and processes can interpret it consistently. For instance, ensuring all country names are recorded as ISO 2-letter codes ("US" instead of "United States" or "U.S.A."), or standardizing date formats across all systems (YYYY-MM-DD). Standardization removes variation and ambiguity. Also, when every team agrees that a "zip code" must be five digits or that "USD" is the default currency, you eliminate obvious errors and reduce the need for downstream validation rules. It's often the first step in a broader data quality pipeline.

- **Data enrichment**: Enrichment makes your data more comprehensive and provides deeper insights. This involves adding valuable, *new* information to existing data, typically from external or internal sources, to enhance data completeness and usefulness. For example, appending geolocation data (longitude/latitude) based on an address or linking a customer record to credit scores, social media profiles, or demographics.

- **Data harmonization**: This is the process of bringing data from disparate sources into a common structure or meaning, allowing it to be compared and analyzed as if it originated from a single, unified source. It often involves mapping different terminologies across systems (e.g., "Customer ID" in one system versus "Client_No" in another), merging similar entities, or reconciling conflicting definitions. Harmonization is crucial for building a cohesive, enterprise-wide view of data, such as a single view of the customer or a consolidated financial report that combines data from multiple, previously isolated systems. Harmonization is primarily a core function of Master Data Management (MDM). MDM is a whole different world, but when it comes to data quality, the most common activity includes combating duplication and fragmentation.

Data stewardship

At its core, data stewardship is about assigning accountability for data within specific business domains. Business data stewards are individuals or teams, often from the business side, who are responsible for defining, maintaining, and ensuring the quality of particular data assets. They are the "custodians" (yes, yet another often-confused term) of the data, bridging the gap between technical management and business understanding, and acting as the frontline for data quality. Some organizations also have a parallel role within IT known as 'Technical Data Stewards' who are responsible for writing and implementing DQ rules on core data elements.

Data governance

Think of governance as the operating framework for managing your organization's data assets. It sets the rules of the game, such as defining policies, processes, roles, responsibilities, and the technologies needed to ensure data is trustworthy, secure, compliant, and fit for purpose.

Why data quality matters

Governance is what makes data quality scalable and sustainable. It defines who owns the data, how standards are set, how definitions get approved, what metrics to track, and how issues are escalated or resolved. In a mature setup, data quality isn't a standalone effort; it operates within the broader umbrella of data governance.

When governance teams act as enablers offering practical playbooks, clarity on decision rights, shared tools, and scorecards, they create the structure for consistent, business-aligned data quality improvements. But if governance becomes a bottleneck or a checkbox exercise, it slows everything down.

The missing link to business value

Data quality initiatives too often feel like isolated technical exercises, disconnected from the very real business outcomes that are critical to the organization. Without a clear and demonstrable link to business KPIs, data quality efforts are destined to slip down the priority list whenever more urgent business demands arise.

Too frequently, what begins as a holistic ambition for end-to-end data quality devolves into fragmented and siloed projects, perhaps limited to cleansing specific source system records or reformatting csv data for a particular initiative.

Your data quality is not a standalone program; it should never become yet another silo within an already siloed organizational structure.

The perception problem

The questions and confusion surrounding DQ are common, spanning from foundational concepts to strategic execution:

- **Whose responsibility is it, truly?** Is it the exclusive domain of IT, or does the business own a piece of it? Should it be managed by Risk, Operations, or shipped off to third-party service vendors? This lack of clarity regarding where DQ resources and accountability reside leads to widespread misunderstandings, impacting everything from daily operations to budget allocation and overall team visibility.

- **A "nice-to-have" versus a "must-have":** Many still perceive data quality as a desirable but not essential endeavor. It is not on the priority list when businesses discuss any new digital, data, or AI initiatives.

- **Where does the money come from?** Budgets for DQ can be allocated from IT operations, governance, or individual business units. When funding is dispersed, initiatives tend to stall. Stakeholders ask: "Why should *I* pay for DQ?" Unless DQ is explicitly tied to Key Performance Indicators (KPIs), such as cost savings, risk reduction, or revenue impact, no one feels compelled to allocate resources.

- **The overwhelming landscape:** Beyond ownership, the sheer volume of evolving technologies and approaches— from data observability and data contracts to DQ testing, monitoring, and the latest buzz around GenAI for modernization can feel overwhelming. *Should you focus on data quality or data observability? Should you use*

GenAI to modernize our DQ? These questions are perfectly normal; it's common for organizations to feel a bit lost or behind in the vast ecosystem of DQ.

The truth is, this confusion often stems from the absence of a clear, compelling answer to one fundamental question: *What does data quality truly mean to your business?* Without that concrete connection, DQ can sometimes also feel like a "Fear Of Missing Out" (FOMO) play; investing because others are, rather than because it addresses a specific, vital business need.

So, why does data quality matter to the business?

"We need to focus on business outcomes"! We have heard this statement multiple times across forums, yet it lacks stickiness within organizations.

When business leaders ask, *"Why should I care about data quality?,"* the answer lies in how it supports what they care about the most. Good data doesn't just clean up reports, it fuels the very engine of business performance.

You might wonder, *"Isn't data quality really an IT or data-team problem? Why should the business get involved?"* After all, developers build pipelines, data engineers write rules, and analysts run reports. It's hardly a bottleneck for business, so why must a business executive concern themselves with row counts or validation failures? Because poor data quality hits the bottom line far more directly than most people realize. Here are the key reasons why data quality should be a top priority for any business leader:

- **Fueling new business use cases**: Initiatives like digital supply chains, e-commerce expansions, or AI-driven operations hinge on integrated data streams. Any break in data quality stalls the entire transformation. With real-time dashboards and self-service analytics, decision cycles have shortened dramatically. Business leaders can no longer wait weeks for the data team to debug pipelines. Reliable, consistent data enables innovation. Whether it's launching a new AI-driven product or a simple data dashboard, clean input data lays the foundation for new capabilities and faster go-to-market strategies.

- **Enhancing customer experience and reducing frustration for internal team**s: Accurate data reduces friction across customer touchpoints, leading to better customer experience, such as fewer duplicate emails and faster service resolutions. Internally, it reduces the time employees spend resolving issues with bad data, providing a single location to access customer data, and allowing them to focus on value-added tasks.

- **Strengthening reliability of existing operational business processes**: Clean data improves process stability and trust in your underlying business processes. Often, consistent bad data forces business teams to change their processes in operational source systems; for example, data collection flows in ERP systems, and it's not an easy job to do. When your source data is trustworthy and clean, downstream business workflows, from supply chain to finance, run with fewer delays, rework, and surprises. This means quicker decisions and improved delivery speed.

- **Minimizing deviations in privacy, risk, and security management:** When compliance officers or risk managers flag an issue, it forces a business-wide scramble and sometimes public disclosure. The cost isn't just financial; it's also a blow to shareholder trust and brand integrity. High-quality data supports a robust compliance posture, enabling organizations to respond to audits, manage risk, and safeguard their reputation more effectively.

- **Boosting business credibility and competitive advantage:** When a customer encounters contradictory data like, "Your online portal says your order shipped yesterday, but our call center shows no record," their trust vanishes. In competitive markets, regaining that trust is often impossible. Internally, trusted data builds confidence in reports and decisions. Externally, accurate customer data leads to personalized experiences, fewer errors, and ultimately, higher customer satisfaction and loyalty. Data quality has a direct impact on your brand reputation.

Data quality won't remain a "nice-to-have" for long; it is rapidly becoming a **must-have**. In the coming years, organizations that proactively adopt efficient methods for managing and governing their data will undoubtedly lead the way, both in terms of revenue growth and delivering superior customer experiences.

---

*It's important to distinguish between **managing DQ** and **resolving DQ** issues. Data quality should be continuously tracked and managed at all levels across the data flow chain. However, for actual systemic improvement, data quality issues should ideally be resolved at their source to prevent them from resurfacing downstream. While this approach is not always immediately feasible, this should be the ultimate goal.*

The aim should be to keep it simple and strategic, making data quality work for us, not the other way around.

Who is "the business" in data quality?

When we talk about involving "the business" in data quality, who exactly do we mean?

It's not just a single person or department. When we speak of "the business" in the context of data quality, we often envision leaders demanding reports or executives requesting KPIs. But business stakeholders influence data quality at **every stage of the data lifecycle,** whether they realize it or not. Broadly, business stakeholders engage with data in three primary capacities:

- **As data producers:** Business teams define and drive operational processes in systems like CRMs, ERPs, and finance tools. Every dropdown, free-text field, and manual entry defines how data is created and what quality issues might emerge downstream.

- **As data transformers:** Business logic shapes how raw data becomes meaningful insight (customer segments, P&L groupings, or compliance thresholds). These aren't just ETL steps; they reflect business understanding that transforms data into decision-ready formats.

- **As data consumers:** Ultimately, business users across all departments are the primary beneficiaries (or sufferers) of data quality. Business users, from analysts to CXOs, rely on clean, reliable data to guide daily operations, strategic choices, and innovation efforts. When data is flawed, trust erodes fast.

In smaller organizations, a single stakeholder or a group of stakeholders might wear all three hats. In large enterprises, the roles may be split across multiple teams or functions. Understanding these distinct roles is the first step toward building true shared ownership of data quality across the organization. We will explore this topic in detail in Chapter 4: Law of Unified Data Governance Force.

> *The key takeaway is simple but powerful: "Data quality is everyone's responsibility, but it only works when it's everyone's priority."*

Data quality isn't just a technical hygiene factor or a checkbox on a compliance form. It's a bridge between operations and outcomes, between what's happening in your systems and what's happening in your business.

As we move into the heart of this book, we'll go beyond frameworks and definitions. You'll see how data quality breaks down, not just in code or systems but in behaviors, assumptions, silos, and inaction.

THREE

Law of Data Inaction

Newton's first law:
An object at rest stays at rest, and an object in motion stays in motion unless acted upon by an external force.

First law of Data Quality:
Bad data quality tends to stay bad unless acted upon by the organization.

Law of Data Inaction

Bad data within your organization won't fix itself. It will continue to spread and compound, unless it is acted upon by someone within your organization.

And by someone, if you're expecting the 'business' to take that action, the first step isn't just assigning them a ticket or forwarding a data issue; it's making sure they understand *why* they should care about bad data quality in the first place.

- Why should businesses prioritize fixing bad quality data?
- What impact does it have on their everyday decisions, workflows, and outcomes?
- How does it affect their business objectives— profitability, efficiency, compliance, or customer satisfaction?

Once they understand the impact of bad data on their business, and by extension, their success, they are far more likely to understand and engage with data quality. But communicating this hasn't always been easy for organizations.

The idea sounds simple. Help the business see the impact, and they'll come on board. But in practice, many organizations struggle with this step. Not because the intent is missing but because stakeholders aren't just decision-makers—**they're people.** And people don't change behavior just because a dashboard says they should.

That's why making the case for data quality isn't only about explaining the "why." It's also about navigating resistance, building ownership, and ultimately, driving action. Because without meaningful follow-through, even the most compelling rationale will fail to create change.

In other words, you're not just making a business case, you're challenging human behavior!

Business stakeholders are human, too!

It's easy to assume that business leaders are just being difficult when they resist data quality initiatives. But the reality is much simpler—they're human, just like the rest of us. They aren't waking up every morning thinking about data integrity, lineage gaps, or data quality rules. Instead, they're focused on meeting their quarterly targets, managing pressures from their bosses, or keeping their teams on track.

Their world is also full of competing priorities. Some are focused on driving revenue growth, others on optimizing costs, and some on improving customer retention. Now, imagine walking into their office and telling them, *"Hey, you need to take ownership of data and start fixing these data quality issues."*

It's no surprise that their first reaction is resistance.

Their reluctance doesn't mean they don't care. It doesn't mean they don't understand the value of clean, reliable data. Often, it means:

- They don't see how data quality connects to their daily work.
- They aren't convinced that fixing it is their responsibility.
- They don't know what specific actions they should take to improve it.

Once they recognize the direct connection between data quality and business success, they'll no longer see it as just another IT initiative. They'll see it as something that affects their targets, performance, and bottom line. And when that happens, data quality stops being an isolated concern and becomes a shared responsibility.

This is where IT and data teams must step up; not just by enforcing rules, but by effectively communicating the *why* of data quality in ways that directly connect to business concerns. And there are countless ways to do this.

How does data quality impact business success?

The key to getting business leaders to care about data quality is simple: connect it to what matters most to them.

Start by analyzing the core business model of each function, its key reason for existence within the organization. If you can demonstrate how bad data hinders their objectives, they'll start paying attention. Here are some examples from my career:

- **Sales and marketing leaders:** The Head of Sales notices that customers are getting bombarded with duplicate, irrelevant marketing emails, leading to unsubscribes, complaints, and may be lost revenue. Why is this happening?

- **Operations and logistics leaders:** The COO has been given a mandate to reduce operational expenses and improve efficiency. They request a dashboard to track process inefficiencies, but IT tells them it will take six weeks to build. Why the delay?

- **Compliance and risk leaders:** The Compliance Officer is concerned about upcoming regulations and potential fines. They see major inconsistencies in how different business units report compliance data. Why is this happening?

- **Technology and IT leaders:** The CTO is struggling with ballooning IT expenses and increasing data storage costs, but can't pinpoint the root cause. Why is IT spending spiraling out of control?

At the heart of every one of these issues is the same root cause: **bad data and delayed action.**

Business leaders will start worrying about data quality when they see how it affects what they already care about.

- If customer data is duplicated, incomplete, or outdated across systems and it is hurting sales conversions, the Head of Sales needs to know.

- If the underlying data is inconsistent, scattered, and requires heavy manual cleanup before reporting, and it is slowing down operations, the COO must understand the cost of inefficiency.

- If data inconsistencies are leading to regulatory fines, the CFO should see the financial risk.

- If poor data governance and management are leading to unnecessary cloud storage costs, the CTO must understand the tech redundancy risk.

I can share another personal example on this:

Think of the airline app you use to check in. On my recent trip with a leading British carrier, their mobile app guided me through a long form to update my personal details and issue my boarding pass; annoying, but manageable. Yet on my return flight, the same app forced me to repeat every field—passport number, contact information, and meal preference—exactly as before.

As a customer, this felt frustrating and unnecessary. I found myself questioning whether I'd ever fly with that airline again. But from a data-quality perspective, it's a perfect case study:

- **Disconnected systems:** No single source of truth for passenger data, so every touchpoint asks for the same information.

- **Duplicate data entry:** Customers waste time repeating the same fields, increasing the chance of typos and mismatches.

- **No centralized customer view:** The business misses opportunities for personalized service, loyalty incentives, or proactive alerts.

This example illustrates how poor data management can directly erode customer experience and brand loyalty, two key metrics that our business leaders care about most. Frustrated customers equal lost revenue and negative word of mouth.

Relate it to their processes and customers, and you'll have business support for your data quality initiatives in no time.

Once business leaders understand that data quality isn't an abstract concept but a direct business enabler, they'll start seeing it as a priority. Your job is to help them connect these dots.

IT and Data Teams	Business Teams
"We need better data governance."	"We need to grow revenue and reduce costs."
"We should implement data quality rules."	"Why is our dashboard delayed again?"
"Let's standardize naming conventions."	"Why are our reports conflicting?"
"Let's implement a data quality tool."	"Why are customers receiving duplicate emails?"

Why inaction feels easier than action

It's essential to understand that answering the question, *Why should I care about data quality?* might not be the only step to achieve data quality engagement. Knowing that something matters doesn't always lead to taking action, especially when the required action feels uncertain, uncomfortable, or disruptive. And that's where things get tricky. You don't just need to communicate the benefits of data quality; you also need to help businesses confront the ill effects of inaction.

In many organizations, inaction isn't just a delay. It quietly becomes the default mindset. Not because businesses don't care, but because human behavior and organizational dynamics naturally resist change. When business leaders don't act on known data issues, the organization adapts, but in all the wrong ways. Workarounds become standard operating procedures. Broken processes get patched instead of repaired. IT and data teams avoid raising issues that might trigger uncomfortable conversations. Data problems are normalized, not fixed. And slowly, a subtle yet powerful narrative sets in:

"This is just how it works around here."

I've seen the same default patterns repeat across companies and roles, and they're almost always rooted in business behavior, not technology:

- **"We've always done it this way"**: A legacy mindset dressed as efficiency.

- **Decision fatigue**: Too many choices, so the safest one becomes no choice at all.

- **"Not my job" syndrome**: Everyone owns data, which too often means no one owns it.

- **Fear of exposure**: Surfacing data issues could reveal upstream flaws, broken processes, or even performance gaps.

Inaction on data doesn't always need to be dramatic; it can also be quiet, slow, and deeply embedded in day-to-day activities. It can also show up as:

- A report takes two weeks to publish, not because analysis is hard but because someone is always fixing last-minute data errors.

- A senior executive questions the accuracy of a dashboard and asks for a version "from someone they trust more." In my discussions, I found that most business units have someone as the go-to person for any data-related questions.

- A project that should have launched last quarter is still stalled, not due to strategy, but because no one can agree on the right dataset.

- Your best analyst spends 60% of their time in Excel, cleaning the same fields over and over again.

- Data terms get defined and redefined—every time someone changes roles.

Over time, all of this creates a culture where inaction feels safer than action. It's similar to how people avoid going to doctors to avoid hearing bad news, even though it's worse to delay.

Left unchecked, this mindset becomes ingrained in the culture. Business teams stop questioning unreliable dashboards. They assign blame to the system or another team. Instead, they default to fixes like manual corrections, parallel spreadsheets, or asking that one person who always cleans it up. You'll hear phrases like:

"This is just how our data works."
"Oh yeah, that report always needs manual cleanup."
"We've got someone in IT who handles that mess."

These are not just symptoms of poor data. They're signals that inaction has become normalized. The longer you live with broken data, the more normal it becomes. And when that happens, even the best tools or governance frameworks can't help because what you're fighting isn't just bad data. You're fighting cultural inertia.

Remember, cultural inaction is far more dangerous than technical debt because it's invisible, unchallenged, and quietly self-reinforcing.

The Business Awakening Curve

To truly shift this from the culture of inaction, business stakeholders need more than an awareness of data quality. Hence, the data and IT teams must guide the business stakeholders through a mindset evolution—one I call **The Business Awakening Curve.**

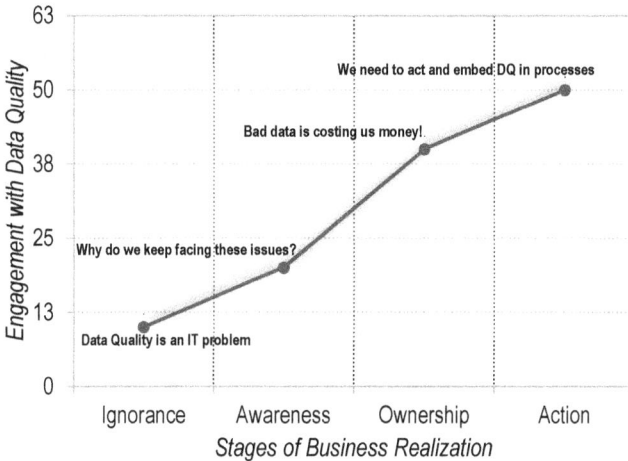

This curve illustrates how organizations, and more specifically, their business stakeholders, come to terms with the reality of data quality. It's not a tech maturity model. It's a human one. It shows the emotional and cognitive journey that the business side of the house often takes from complete detachment to deep ownership. It emphasizes that business engagement with data quality usually evolves not in a single leap, but across various stages of realization.

There are four stages of this realization:

Ignorance

This is where it all starts. In this stage, data quality is often seen as an IT or Ops problem. Business leaders might acknowledge that data is important, but they don't see it as their responsibility.

Reports don't add up? Blame the dashboard. Numbers don't make sense? Talk to the data team. There's little accountability, and almost no engagement. The cost of bad data is invisible or worse, accepted as the price of doing business.

"That's a data issue, not my issue" kind of mindset is commonly seen at this stage.

Awareness

Something shifts. A high-stakes decision goes wrong, a customer complaint reveals broken data, or a manual process starts draining time and energy.

Now, the business might start to see the impact of poor data quality if it's communicated properly, but they're not yet sure what to do about it. Common questions that emerge are:

"Why does this keep happening?"
"Who owns this data?"
"Why isn't it fixed already?"

This is often a critical turning point because it's where blame can either turn inward (constructively) or back outward (defensively). Unfortunately, I find many organizations stay stuck here, circling the problem but never stepping into it.

"We know there's a problem...but it's still not our job to solve it" kind of mindset is common at this stage.

Ownership

This is the most common stage that many organizations are investing in and trying to reach. Entire federated data governance is aimed at this stage (more on that in the next chapter). Here, the business usually stops pointing fingers and starts taking responsibility. Leaders begin to understand that data problems are, in fact, business problems. They realize that if sales works off the wrong customer segments, or if finance can't reconcile numbers, it's not just a systems glitch, it's a strategic risk!

At this stage, business teams begin collaborating more closely with data and IT counterparts. They ask better questions. They challenge their own processes. They begin to assign clear owners to data-critical workflows. Importantly, they start seeing data quality as something that lives inside their function—not just adjacent to it.

"This affects our outcomes. We need to fix it." You can see the mindset evolving towards action.

Action

This is the true north star for organizations where meaningful change happens. Data quality becomes embedded in everyday operations. Business teams don't just react to issues; they proactively design processes, tools, and checkpoints to prevent them. DQ is no longer just a side conversation or a post-mortem talking point. It's a living part of the business process flow included in KPIs, tracked during planning, and seen as a shared responsibility.

At this stage, the entire organization aligns around the idea that good decisions start with good data and that acting on data quality is not a one-time project, but an ongoing discipline.

"We don't just care about data quality—we act on it." The true north star mindset!

Being stuck in any stage before action means the organization is still vulnerable. Awareness without ownership leads to endless loops of frustration. Ownership without action fosters cynicism. Even well-meaning conversations can become comforting traps that prevent real change.

The approach to "sell" data quality just by explaining its value is not sufficient. The real work, the cultural shift, often lies in guiding business stakeholders through this curve. Sometimes that means surfacing uncomfortable truths. At other times, it's about showing the cost of doing nothing. But the goal is always to keep the journey moving forward. Because if we stop short of action, nothing much really changes.

Action leads to motivation. Not the other way around.
Good data doesn't happen by default. It happens by
deliberate action.

FOUR

Law of
Unified Data Governance Force

Newton's second law:
The force acting on an object is equal to the mass of the
object times its acceleration (F = ma).

Second law of Data Quality:
The bigger the data quality problem (mass), the greater the
effort (force) required to achieve meaningful improvement
(acceleration).

Federated or fragmented governance?

In recent years, many organizations have adopted concepts like federated data governance and decentralized data ownership, often inspired by frameworks such as the data mesh. These approaches promise agility, domain ownership, and scalability.

And, naturally, data quality becomes a part of this federated vision. Unfortunately, in the name of decentralization, data governance and data quality have become siloed pillars within organizations themselves.

My current employer, Thoughtworks Inc., is a company that has been at the forefront of the entire Data Mesh framework, which includes federated governance. Since joining the company in 2024, I've had the opportunity to delve deeper into the philosophy and the limitations of these models. And I've come to realize something unfortunate: many organizations, conference talks, and research publications have misunderstood the foundational intent of federation. What was meant to foster collaboration and autonomy has, in many cases, led to fragmentation and duplication. It's critical to understand that:

---

*Federated governance doesn't mean
fragmented governance.*

It doesn't mean each business unit should develop its own processes, tools, and standards in isolation. Rather, it means that while each domain can prioritize its business problems and act on them independently, the core governance foundation—tools, policies, and platforms must remain connected and coordinated.

Take a data catalog, for example. If every unit implements its own, how do you expect to build an enterprise-wide data view? Or if each team defines its own data quality metrics in silos, how can you ensure consistency, traceability, or reuse across the organization?

This misunderstanding is one of the primary reasons why data silos persist, despite decades of efforts to eliminate them. We've just reinvented them under new terminology.

To improve data quality at scale, we must stop pretending that individual teams can solve it alone. The only real force strong enough to drive change is one that's created together. And that's where the Law of Unified Data Governance Force comes in!

The Law of Unified Data Governance Force

So, what does the second law of unified data governance force say?

"The larger the data quality problem (mass), the greater the effort (force) required to achieve meaningful improvement (acceleration)—and that improvement cannot occur without alignment, sponsorship, support, accountability, and the right tools."

In short, the Effort required to fix DQ = Size of the issue (mass) × Acceleration (rate of improvement), where Acceleration = Alignment × Sponsorship × Support × Accountability × Tools.

Let me try to break that down further:

- Mass = The scale, complexity, and business impact of the data issue. Some DQ problems are minor annoyances. Others undermine entire business processes, pose regulatory risks, or result in millions of dollars in lost revenue.

- Force = The real-world effort, time, cost, and people's collective will that is required to resolve the issue.

- Acceleration = The speed and momentum of improvement, driven by cross-functional collaboration that includes alignment from business teams, support from executives and data governance groups, shared accountability, and delivery from IT and data teams.

The formula premise is simple:
big problems require big force.

And yet in most organizations, this equation is completely ignored. Large-scale data issues are often handed to a single team, typically IT or data, without the necessary business context, sponsorship, or cross-functional support to effectively address them. In that setup, acceleration is close to zero. And with zero acceleration, no matter how big the problem, the force (i.e., real change) never materializes. To solve this, I spent time speaking with experts across industries and learned that:

Centralization alone doesn't scale, and pure
decentralization leads to fragmentation.

Organizations need a model that enables autonomy but still amplifies collaboration. Federated data governance is a necessity for many. No single central team can handle the growing complexity, speed, and scale of enterprise data on its own. And add AI on top of this to further complicate things.

The Core-Hub Approach

My interactions and research showed that companies that excel at mesh or federation have a well-functioning federated governance operating model that relies on a firm, central core—a governance or data management hub (data quality inclusive) that supports, connects, and accelerates the work of distributed hubs, specifically the individual business units and domains. I have also attempted to create a simple replica of what that model resembles in many organizations today.

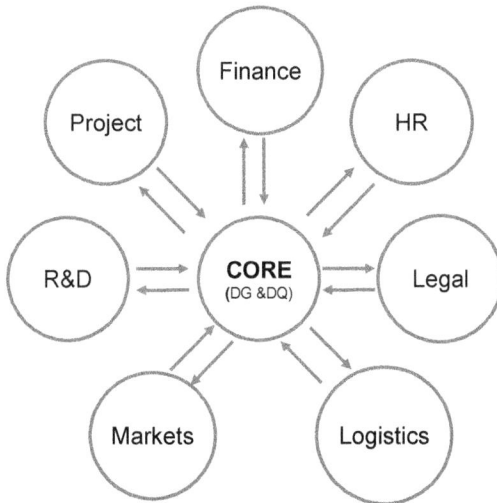

In this model:

- At the center sits the core governance or data management team. Their responsibility is not to control anything, but to enable everything. They provide:

- Common policies and principles

- A shared toolkit of platforms and processes

- Clear definitions for data standards and metrics

- A single source of alignment across all domains

- Additionally, this core can also include your data platforms and associated layers based on the flexibility needs.

Think of them as the architects of your data ecosystem. They don't build every part of the house, but they make sure it stands on a stable foundation and follows a unified blueprint.

The hubs are formed around each key business area, such as Finance, HR, R&D, Legal, and Logistics, empowered to drive local decision-making and each with its own data team experts that:

- Prioritizes local use cases
- Handles day-to-day data stewardship activities that involve the implementation of domain-level data quality controls

- Adheres to the core's standards while adapting them to local needs
- Feeds operational insights and challenges back into the core.

What's critical is that this autonomy is not absolute. The hubs are closely tied to the core, not just in terms of results, but also in how they achieve those results.

If domains are given freedom without guidance, it usually leads to fragmentation, duplicated efforts, and incompatible definitions of truth. In short, your federation models break.

The links between core and hubs are critical. This is not a one-way chain of command. It represents a two-way collaboration for shared accountability, reusable processes, and continuous support. This balance of autonomy and alignment allows for both innovation and control—a rare combination in large organizations.

What if a domain is too large or complex to manage through a single hub? That's where nested governance comes in. Hubs can create their own sub-units, essentially smaller data teams that handle specific functions or regions, while still reporting to the main hub and adhering to the standards from the core.

This layered structure is what makes the model scalable. It's not a flat organization. It's fractal—the same pattern repeats at every level, keeping governance both flexible and grounded.

Without this core, the hubs become disconnected. Each domain ends up reinventing the wheel. Teams choose different tools, build separate workflows, and measure success in inconsistent ways. Eventually, silos take hold. Efforts are duplicated, trust depreciates, and the organization loses the very thing data governance is meant to protect: a shared version of truth.

To illustrate this with an example, although it may be a cliché, consider how global airlines operate. The central control tower at an international airport doesn't fly the planes. But it coordinates their movements, manages the airspace, ensures all aircraft follow the same flight paths and safety standards, and communicates continuously with each pilot. Each plane has autonomy in how it flies, but without that control tower, the entire system would descend into chaos. Similarly, the core-and-hub model of data governance ensures that while each business unit navigates its own journey, they all remain aligned with a central plan, thereby avoiding collisions and delays in the organization's broader data transformation efforts.

This model is not just about structure; it is about creating a scalable, connected, and sustainable foundation for enterprise-wide data governance and quality.

How to avoid data quality becoming a silo?

Let's now turn to a critical question: how do we ensure that this structure doesn't simply create new silos? If the promise of federated data governance and quality is to be truly realized, unseen walls between business and centralized teams must come down. These two entities are not meant to operate in separate vacuums; instead, they must work in seamless collaboration to conquer business challenges. This critical interplay is visually represented in what I term the "Data Quality Partnership Matrix," which underscores the vital balance needed to break free from DQ silos.

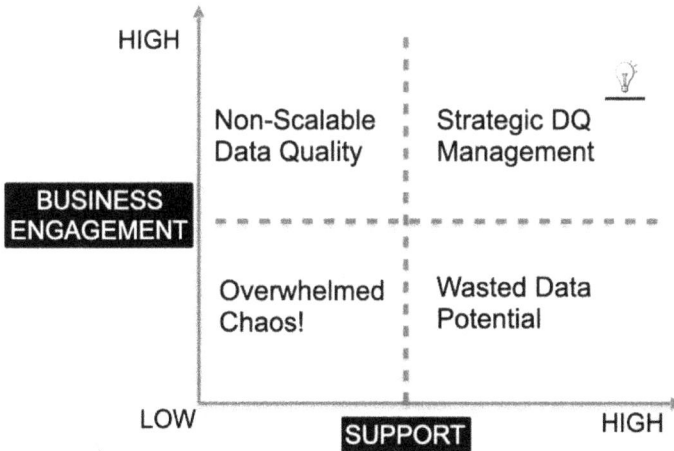

No matter how skilled your IT team is, how passionate your data stewards are, or how invested a few business leaders might be, **data quality cannot be improved in isolation**. Like physics, it takes a combination of variables to move the needle. In the enterprise world, this means partnership.

- **X-axis: support:** This represents the extent to which the central data governance or data quality teams provide education, communication, standards alignment, and tools to the business counterparts to manage and improve data quality.

- **Y-axis: business engagement:** This signifies the level of involvement, ownership, understanding, and active participation of business stakeholders in data quality initiatives.

1. Low business engagement, low support: overwhelmed chaos!

This is the worst scenario. In this state, business teams are likely struggling with poor data quality that affects their operations and decision-making. However, there's little to no guidance, training, communication, standardized tools, or alignment on standards from a central data governance or quality function. Simultaneously, the business may not fully recognize the impact of poor data or feel empowered to address it. Data quality issues go unnoticed or are ignored, leading to poor decision-making, inefficiencies, and possibly significant compliance or regulatory risks.

For example, marketing campaigns often suffer from inaccurate segmentation due to incomplete or outdated customer data. The marketing team blames IT or the data teams for "bad data." At the same time, IT lacks business context to understand the specific data quality issues, and there's no formal process for reporting or resolving them. Eventually, bad data remains in that state for a long time, as there is no ownership involved to resolve the issues.

2. High business engagement, low support: non-scalable data quality

A common quadrant for most companies today. In this quadrant, business teams are highly aware of and concerned about data quality issues. They might even be proactively trying to fix problems within their domains. However, the lack of central support in terms of education, communication of best practices, alignment on standards, and provision of practical tools, limits their ability to implement scalable and consistent solutions.

As a result, the business is forced to bear a heavy burden in managing DQ on its own, which may lead to burnout, inefficiencies, and localized fixes that don't address the root causes or integrate well across the organization. This is where you'll see the 'Shift Left' phenomenon widely discussed and propagated by business teams, basically because the business teams are tired of temporary solutions to fix data and want to pass on the responsibility to source teams from where the data originates. I will discuss it further in the upcoming chapters.

For example, a product development team tries to manage product data on its own, meticulously tracks and corrects data inconsistencies in its product specifications using spreadsheets, but these efforts aren't aligned with how the same data is managed in other systems (e.g., manufacturing, sales) due to a lack of central data standards and communication. They spend excessive time manually cleaning up spreadsheets, which diverts them from their core responsibilities. Product teams, therefore, become overwhelmed and frustrated as they attempt to handle DQ without proper support, resulting in a lack of scalability and potential degradation of data quality over time.

3. Low business engagement, high support: wasted data potential

Another prevalent situation involves organizations heavily investing in data governance and quality initiatives, often outsourcing these efforts to external IT or consultancy firms, which are expected to manage poor data within day-to-day operations.

In these cases, central data governance or data quality teams often invest heavily in sophisticated tools without assessing core business needs, and many also launch extensive training programs through Learning and Development, as well as align technical processes with source systems. On paper, the support structure looks strong. But there's one critical flaw—business teams are not genuinely engaged. They either do not fully understand the importance of the initiatives or fail to see enough value to change their day-to-day behavior.

As a result, resources are underutilized, and improvements often fall short of their mark. The data quality efforts usually end up solving technical problems without addressing the real business pain points. Over time, this disconnect not only wastes valuable investment but can also reinforce silos due to a lack of shared ownership and accountability.

For example, an organization rolls out a sophisticated data catalog and data quality monitoring system. The governance team also creates detailed training modules and conducts workshops. However, business users rarely interact with the platform, resist altering their daily workflows, and often view governance processes as irrelevant overhead. Without active business participation, the well-supported infrastructure fails to tackle the most pressing data quality issues, ultimately leading to poor adoption and low impact from the DQ programs.

4. High business engagement, high support: strategic data quality management

This is the ideal state. Both business and governance teams are fully engaged and supportive of data quality initiatives. Business users actively participate in identifying and communicating quality issues, providing remediation guidance, and improving processes. Meanwhile, centralized governance functions provide the necessary frameworks, tools, training, and coordination to scale these efforts across the organization.

The result is a strategic, business-aligned data quality management practice that drives real value, thus improving decision-making, operational efficiency, and regulatory compliance. Importantly, this environment fosters true collaboration rather than ownership battles. Data quality becomes everyone's responsibility, embedded naturally into daily processes rather than seen as an external imposition.

For example, a financial services firm establishes a governance framework that enables business domain leads to work closely with central governance teams. Business units are responsible for defining critical data elements and setting quality thresholds, while the central team provides stewardship platforms, monitoring tools, escalation workflows, and ongoing training. When issues arise, they are jointly triaged based on their business impact. As a result, data-driven decision-making improves significantly, regulatory audits become easier to manage, and customer trust strengthens over time.

In the end, true data quality excellence requires not just strong tools or passionate teams in isolation, but a partnership where business engagement and central support work in tandem— consistently, transparently, and strategically.

Why data quality acceleration remains low

Earlier, we discussed 'Support' in the context of the DQ Partnership Matrix, but support from the data governance or quality team alone isn't enough to drive sustainable momentum. To truly accelerate the rate of data quality improvement across an organization, several other foundational factors must come into play.

Let's revisit our equation:

Effort required to fix DQ = Size of the issue (mass) ×
Acceleration (rate of improvement)
where:
Acceleration = Alignment × Sponsorship × Support ×
Accountability × Tools

Just as friction in physics resists motion, certain organizational frictions resist data quality acceleration even when significant effort (force) is applied. If any of the five acceleration factors above is close to zero, the entire momentum collapses. Despite ambitious roadmaps, significant investments in tools, and growing executive awareness, many organizations still struggle to make meaningful progress, often achieving only marginal or unsustainable gains. Why?

Because acceleration in data quality is not just about more resources. It depends on the synergy of strategy alignment, shared responsibility, leadership, technology, and enablement. When these elements are missing, data quality programs remain fragmented and fail to scale, leaving organizations with persistent data challenges. Below are the core "friction points" that silently stall progress:

1. **The void of shared accountability:** When no clear end-to-end accountability exists for data quality, issues are addressed tactically rather than systemically. Business teams assume it's an IT problem. IT assumes it's a governance problem. And governance often lacks the authority to enforce change. The broader organization doesn't feel truly accountable for the data it produces, transforms, or consumes. Relying on implicit ownership or "someone will pick it up" guarantees that nobody will. As responsibility diffuses, so does the urgency and will to act.

2. **Alignment gaps:** Acceleration demands directional clarity, but most organizations suffer from competing agendas. Alignment gaps occur when business priorities, IT roadmaps, and governance objectives are not fully aligned. Teams pursue local targets, such as sales teams chasing revenue, IT teams focusing on feature delivery or platform migration, and governance teams pursuing compliance. Everyone moves, but not in the same direction. Without a shared understanding of which data quality issues matter most and why, effort is scattered and the impact is diluted. Without shared goals, every push works at cross-purposes.

3. **Governance as bottleneck, not enabler:** The general perception of data governance often hinders rather than supports the acceleration of data quality. In many organizations, data governance is still primarily viewed as a control function focused solely on risk, privacy, and compliance. And when they start acting like gatekeepers, prioritizing control and compliance over collaboration, they can slow down both innovation and the implementation of data quality improvements. Instead of empowering domains, they become the very chokepoint that stifles acceleration. As discussed in the DQ Partnership Matrix, governance must provide frameworks, guidance, and tools that enable domains to own and improve their data quality, rather than feeling restricted by it.

4. **Under-leveraged tools and support gaps:** Tooling is not a silver bullet, we all agree. Many companies fall into one of two traps: (a) platforms are underutilized because users aren't trained or supported, or (b) platforms are used as dumping grounds flooded with information, but disconnected from any business value or resolution process. Even the best data-quality platforms fail to accelerate change if users lack training, support, or clear processes for remediation. Tools without hands-on guidance become expensive shelfware.

5. **Superficial sponsorship:** And last but not least, the absence of strong sponsorship. Weak sponsorship is

evident when executives discuss data quality but fail to allocate time, budget, or visible recognition. A one-time funding announcement or an occasional mention in a slide deck does little to overcome everyday emergencies. When leadership fails to reinforce DQ as a strategic imperative, teams default back to their functional priorities.

What about culture? Isn't that the root cause of all these challenges?

Yes and No. **Culture is the sum of everything described above.**

It's not a separate point; it's embedded in all of them. Culture is shaped by shared accountability, leadership modeling, consistent alignment, training, and reinforcement. So rather than isolating it as a standalone barrier, I've woven it through the above factors because every one of these frictions is cultural at its core.

Achieving meaningful acceleration with the fit-for-purpose mindset

Acceleration requires focus!

Acceleration in data quality comes not from trying to fix every issue at once, but from concentrating effort where it truly matters.

Data quality acceleration is defined as:

$$Acceleration = Alignment \times Sponsorship \times Support \times Accountability \times Tools$$

All factors on the right—strong alignment with business goals, executive sponsorship, robust support, clear accountability, and capable tools are essential. Yet if the "scope" is infinite, your "mass" of issues becomes too great to overcome, and no amount of force can generate real acceleration.

Instead, it's critical to adopt a **Fit-for-Purpose mindset,** focusing exclusively on the data that drives decisions, revenue, and risk mitigation, and then iterate outward from there.

Thoughts from Dr. Sebastian Wernicke, author of the best-selling book "Data Inspired," highly resonated with me.[1]

Dr. Sebastian Wernicke aptly highlights that data initiatives often stall not because data is unavailable or unclean, but because priorities are unclear. You can polish dozens of tables and mend countless technical discrepancies. Still, if the sales team, for example, remains incentivized solely to chase monthly quotas rather than cultivate long-term customer relationships, no amount of "perfect data" will fundamentally change their behavior or their outcomes.

---

[1] https://www.linkedin.com/feed/update/urn:li:activity:7331963303067385856/.

Data is too often treated as the main character in the business narrative, when its true power lies in being a supporting player. Data only creates tangible value when it drives decisions and revenue, not merely because a dashboard exists or a quality rule is met.

Consider the ideal sequence for value creation:

Strategy → Decisions → Data Needed → Analysis

Too many organizations operate in reverse:

Data → Dashboards → Decisions (never come)

They start by gathering vast amounts of data, building impressive dashboards, and then passively hope that complex business problems will somehow resolve themselves. It's no wonder those dashboards end up gathering dust, disconnected from the very strategic questions they were meant to inform.

The fit-for-purpose philosophy channels effort precisely where it will yield the greatest impact, ensuring that data is "good enough" for its intended use and directly supports the most pressing business needs.

How, then, should we identify what truly matters to the business and apply this mindset effectively? I believe these approaches are useful:

1. **Start with real business challenges:** We discussed this earlier. Begin by identifying the genuinely pressing issues that keep your leadership awake at night; whether it's shrinking profit margins, accelerating customer churn, persistent supply-chain disruptions, or looming compliance gaps. These are the strategic pain points that demand immediate action and where data quality improvements will yield the most visible results.

2. **Define the data you truly need to support business outcomes:** Once you have a crystal-clear understanding of the business problem, reverse-engineer the data requirements. Do you need highly accurate customer lifetime value data to improve retention? Or impeccably clean product-cost data to protect profit margins? Focus your data quality efforts on those specific tables and fields first. Rigorously ignore everything else until these critical elements are addressed and deliver value.

3. **Empower domain experts to drive strategy:** Actively hire or involve individuals who possess deep, nuanced understanding of your business operations. Empower them to lead the conversation, articulating: "Here's exactly how our invoicing process works; here's precisely where data errors matter most for our close." Their invaluable domain expertise ensures that you don't waste precious cycles on low-impact data issues, instead directing "force" to where it genuinely matters (more on these experts in the Engagement mantras chapter).

4. **Measure success by changed decisions, not perfect dashboards:** Shift your success metrics. Instead of simply tracking "dashboards delivered on time," measure whether daily business decisions are tangibly shifting. Did the marketing team send fewer emails to invalid addresses? Did finance close the books faster because invoice accuracy improved? Did the billing dispute rate drop? These outcome-driven metrics are what truly fuel momentum and sponsorship, far more than polished visuals ever can.

5. **Iterate and expand:** Once a high-impact use case is successfully producing tangible results and demonstrating clear Return on Investment (ROI), celebrate that win. Then, strategically utilize the assets created in this use case to address the following prioritized challenge. Build a clear roadmap of "business-first" data improvements, each tied to a specific decision or revenue outcome. Over time, these incremental wins will compound, building enterprise-wide acceleration and fostering a pervasive culture of data quality.

Let's take an example to explain the fit-for-purpose in action. Imagine a large retailer trying to write DQ rules for every attribute in a 10-million-item catalog. That's a massive undertaking (mass = huge) with limited acceleration, implying too much force, too many issues. Now, flip the approach:

- Leadership says: "Our immediate goal is to reduce cart abandonment by ensuring accurate price and availability on our top 10% revenue SKUs."

- The DQ team creates three priority rules for those specific 10% SKUs:

  - Price Validity Rule: Verify that the listed price matches the approved price book.
  - Availability Check Rule: Confirm that "in-stock" status aligns with real-time inventory.
  - Description Completeness Rule: Ensure every SKU has a non-null, standardized description.

By focusing on these three rules for 10% of the items, the "mass" shrinks by 90%.

Within weeks, the retailer sees a **5% increase in conversions, resulting in tangible revenue growth**. That rapid win builds trust and sponsorship for the next priority, such as applying DQ rules to seasonal inventory accuracy, thus maintaining high acceleration rather than diluting it.

By narrowing the scope, you turbocharge the force applied, making acceleration multiply rather than fragment. This targeted, fit-for-purpose approach removes the paralysis of "fix every error everywhere." Instead, it channels your data quality "force" into the highest-value areas, ensuring that your efforts become visible, trusted, and, above all, impactful.

Remember that identifying what matters as 'Fit-for-Purpose' requires a proper approach and a mindset change.

Acceleration must start at the top

Who can remove the data quality friction and truly accelerate the efforts around it?

The answer is clear: senior leadership!

Acceleration is not a grassroots phenomenon. It must be ignited and sustained from the top. Without visible executive commitment, every other effort, no matter how well designed, will slide back into inertia. Leaders can eliminate each friction point and drive real momentum by:

- **Aligning** by setting shared DQ goals alongside revenue, efficiency, and risk metrics.

- **Sponsoring** by funding initiatives, removing organizational roadblocks, and celebrating DQ wins publicly.

- **Supporting** by staffing central governance/help teams, offering hands-on training, and ensuring hubs have timely access to expertise.

- **Holding accountable** by assigning clear owners for critical data domains and tying performance reviews to DQ outcomes.

- **Providing tools** by selecting and continuously refining platforms that integrate seamlessly with both business and technical user needs.

Without this unwavering commitment and clear direction from the top, the organizational system will likely remain in a state of inertia. There will be no significant acceleration in data quality improvement, and as a result, the considerable effort required to fix even well-known and impactful data issues will never truly materialize. Without that top-down commitment, the entire force equation collapses and even the biggest teams cannot move the mass alone.

When leadership actively drives alignment, sponsorship, support, accountability, and tooling, they create the acceleration needed to turn effort into real improvement.

Who should own data quality?

So, does organizational-wide senior leadership own data quality? Or individual business leaders? Or IT? Or data teams?

The pursuit of high-quality data cannot be the sole burden of a single team or department. It touches every phase of the data lifecycle from its initial creation to transformation to eventual consumption. Consequently, its ownership must also be a collective endeavor, a **shared responsibility** embraced by everyone who interacts with data, from data engineers and analysts to business users and leaders.

Crucially, within this ecosystem, business stakeholders are not passive recipients of data; they are active participants across the entire data flow. The business is not an isolated unit in itself; business users play roles as data producers, data transformers, and data consumers, making their understanding, engagement, and ownership of data quality not just important, but foundational.

In most organizations, we can identify three primary ways in which business stakeholders engage with data:

- **1. Business as data producers:** Business users are on the front lines of data creation, setting the stage for data quality. Through operational processes in CRMs, ERPs, and other transactional systems, they define what data gets captured and how in the form of business processes. Their understanding of business rules, customer interactions, and operational needs sets the tone for overall data accuracy and completeness. Some examples include that sales operations defines the customer input protocols in the CRM, supply chain determines how inventory and vendor data is logged, and customer service ensures feedback and support tickets are accurately recorded. If poor data goes in here, no transformation can make it good later.

- **2. Business as data transformers:** Transformation isn't just technical. It's also about business logic, such as segmentation rules, financial rollups, or KPI definitions; shaping the data for specific use. While IT platforms often provide the infrastructure and technical capabilities for data transformation, business stakeholders determine what the data should mean. They are crucial in defining the logic, rules, and aggregations needed to derive meaningful insights. They act as the bridge between raw data and actionable intelligence. Examples include marketing defines how customer segments are constructed, finance shapes consolidation logic for multi-entity reporting, and product teams set the rules for measuring feature adoption. This step is where messy data can become meaningful or stay misunderstood.

- **3. Business as data consumers:** Ultimately, business users across all departments are the primary consumers of data. They rely on reports, dashboards, analytical tools, and increasingly, AI-driven insights to understand performance, identify trends, make strategic decisions, and drive operational improvements. Their ability to trust and effectively utilize this information depends on its quality and relevance. Whether it's a frontline employee viewing a customer profile or a CEO scanning a dashboard, trust in data quality defines the outcome. Examples include executives steering company strategy based on topline metrics, managers tracking performance against goals using reports, and frontline staff using data daily to serve customers, resolve issues, or drive sales. Data that can't be trusted here becomes a liability regardless of how clean it looked upstream.

Data quality ownership often fails due to disconnect

Despite business being involved across all three stages, data quality ownership is often stuck in the 'blame-game' loop, primarily because:

- Data producers don't hear from data consumers.
- Data consumers don't know where the data came from.
- Data transformers respond to narrow business use-case requests, without understanding end-to-end context.

Imagine a crucial 'RevenueValue' column, intended for numerical calculations, begins receiving non-numeric entries such as "Not Applicable," "Pending," or simple dashes from a newly integrated source system. Since the downstream data pipeline is designed to handle flexible types gracefully, it silently converts these into generic strings, preventing immediate errors. A monthly financial forecasting model, however, consumes this seemingly innocuous data. The non-numeric entries quietly skew aggregations, leading to a multi-million-dollar discrepancy in revenue predictions that is only discovered weeks later, after critical business decisions have already been made.

Or consider your analytical data warehouse. The explicit relationships between key tables (e.g., SalesTransactions and CustomerMaster) are not rigorously enforced or monitored. Over time, due to source system changes or load errors, sales records begin to reference customer IDs that no longer exist in the master customer list or reference products that have been retired. This breakdown in keeping those table links accurate (often called "referential integrity") goes unnoticed until a business analyst attempts to build a consolidated report on customer lifetime value, finding that a significant percentage of sales cannot be linked to actual customers, making the dashboard numbers fundamentally unreliable and impossible to reconcile.

> *This structural disconnect across teams is why most data quality initiatives feel fragmented. Issues are fixed tactically, not systematically. Quality problems recur. Ownership is unclear.*

Given the high stakes of revenue, cost, compliance, customer loyalty, AI readiness, and competitive edge, it's clear that data quality cannot live solely in the IT or data realm. It is intrinsically a "shared business imperative." Ignoring data quality is far riskier and more expensive within today's competitive industries.

The business doesn't just sit at the end of the pipeline; it runs through every part of it. When business teams see themselves not only as data consumers but also as stewards of what goes in and how it's shaped, they start to act differently. End-to-end data quality must be collectively owned. Shared ownership isn't about spreading responsibility thin—it's about making accountability visible, aligned, and continuous throughout the entire process. That's how data quality becomes a business capability, not a governance afterthought.

When every group, from the field sales rep to the C-suite executive, understands their part in this chain, data quality stops being "someone else's problem" and becomes a shared business imperative. When business leaders recognize the high stakes, they stop asking, "Should IT handle DQ?" and start asking, "How do we, together, ensure our data fuels our strategy rather than threatens it?"

However, it's crucial to understand that not everyone perceives data in the same way. What matters to one may seem irrelevant to another. And that's where most DQ efforts get lost—**in translation**.

If we want accountability to stick and ownership to scale, we must stop speaking about data quality in a one-size-fits-all language.

That's where Newton's 3rd law helps us!

FIVE

Law of Action versus Reaction

Newton's third law:
For every action, there is an equal and opposite reaction.

Third law of Data Quality:
For every push on technical jargon, business will push back
harder with confusion, frustration and irritation.

Data quality is always contextual

As part of my role, I'm fortunate to attend many data conferences around the world. One particular event, widely attended by C-suite executives, CDAOs, and CIOs from Fortune 500 companies, left a lasting impression on me because the learnings from this conference highlighted a core truth about data quality that is often overlooked.

In the keynote address, a prominent speaker emphasized the foundational role of data in scaling AI initiatives. One line in their presentation stood out to me:

> *"Data quality is the #1 obstacle to implementing AI."*

I nodded in agreement. It made perfect sense. I jotted down a few notes and moved on to the next session.

There, another distinguished expert delivered a talk titled "Common Misconceptions Around AI and Data." This speaker, equally experienced and credible, confidently declared:

> *"High-quality data as a prerequisite for AI readiness is one of the biggest myths."*

For a brief moment, I was genuinely surprised. Two accomplished voices, speaking within the same conference on the same day, were seemingly contradicting each other. But as I reflected further, I realized something critical: **both perspectives are absolutely valid.**

They weren't contradicting each other. They were interpreting "data quality" through entirely different lenses, shaped by their individual experiences, domains, and objectives over decades. And that's precisely the point I've been trying to make for years.

We must stop treating data quality as a
one-size-fits-all concept.

The term 'data quality' means very different things to different people, and trying to define it with a single, rigid framework is a guaranteed way to lose your audience and impact.

- For a compliance officer, data quality might be about regulatory reporting and audit readiness.

- For a supply chain leader, it's accurate inventory levels and timely logistics data.

- For an AI team, it's about complete, structured, labeled data that models can learn from.

- For a sales manager, it might be about having the correct customer data at the right time to close deals.

They're all talking about quality. But they're speaking entirely different dialects.

Whether it is a finance leader, a supply chain director, or a product analyst, each defines "good data" in drastically different ways. Their definitions are shaped by the decisions they make, the risks they face, and the outcomes they prioritize.

Yes, organizations can and should have shared DQ processes, playbooks, and platforms. However, the definition of what constitutes "good data" cannot be universal. It must be contextual.

It must reflect the specific needs, purpose, and pain points of each business function, team, and decision-maker.

And this is where many data quality programs often fail; not because the tools are inadequate or the intent is lacking, but because the language is incorrect. DQ efforts often get **lost in translation**.

If we want accountability to stick and ownership to scale, we must learn to speak data quality in multiple languages.

We must move away from generic definitions and start meeting our stakeholders where they are translating the value of data quality into terms they understand and care about.

And that brings us to the Third Law of Data Quality, where communication becomes just as important as strategy.

Law of action versus reaction

Newton's Third Law of Motion: For every action, there is an equal and opposite reaction.

Our Third Law of Data Quality: For every push of technical jargon, business stakeholders respond with equal and opposite pushback—confusion, frustration, irritation, and eventually, disengagement.

In our First Law of Data Quality (The Law of Data Inaction), we explored '*why*' the business should care about data quality.

In our Second Law (The Law of Unified Data Governance), we focused on '*what*' factors are essential to accelerate data quality efforts and establish ownership of data quality.

Now, the Third Law of Data Quality addresses '*how*' to bring these efforts to life—by communicating data quality in a language the business understands.

And the most fundamental human element of this '*how*' part is: **communication**.

No matter how robust your governance model or how powerful your analytics platforms, your data quality efforts will stall if the people you're speaking with don't understand you or, worse, feel alienated by your communication around the state of data. When technical teams deliver dense, jargon-laden explanations to business leaders, the inevitable response is pushback.

The "action" in this law isn't necessarily a negative one in intent. Technical teams are often driven by the need to be technically precise and thorough in their explanations. However, when this precision comes at the expense of clarity for the business audience, the "reaction" is predictable and counterproductive.

That resistance can look like:

- Dismissing data initiatives as "IT or the data team's problem"

- Ignoring dashboards filled with unfamiliar metrics

- Always relying on a 'special someone' to manually verify the data

- Quietly reverting to outdated spreadsheets and manual workarounds instead of trusting the new system.

Just as a physical object won't move if opposing forces are equal, your data quality program cannot advance if your communication generates equal and opposite resistance.

Why doesn't the business get it?

One of the most common frustrations voiced by IT and data leaders is, *"The business just doesn't get it!"* or *"Data quality is never a priority for our business leaders."*

But have we truly considered the reasons behind this perceived lack of understanding?

At its core, the answer is simple: **it's not their language.**

Nobody teaches federated computational governance in business schools. No sales leader or operations head was ever onboarded with the expectation of learning data quality rules through a highly specialized DQ tool. Business stakeholders weren't trained or hired to monitor null percentages, row count anomalies, or source system latencies.

They just aren't programmed for it.

Often, the issue lies not in the business's inability to comprehend but in our failure to communicate in their language and connect data quality to their core objectives.

As we discussed in Chapter 3, business stakeholders are human, too. They operate under intense pressure to deliver real-world outcomes, including increasing revenue, reducing costs, meeting compliance targets, and retaining customers. Nowhere in their performance metrics does it say, *"Fix upstream data anomalies in the source system."*

And yet, we blame them for not understanding or caring about data quality. Data quality, for them, can feel like an abstract concept, a technical burden that doesn't directly align with their primary responsibilities.

For decades, data quality has been viewed as a technical/IT concern, and yet we still expect the business to grasp its importance instantly. But how can they, if no one has ever translated it into something meaningful, relevant, or actionable in their terms?

Some might argue, *"But our IT/data teams have set up SLAs, data contracts, and real-time alerts. We have even invested in data observability tools. We do notify the business ASAP every time a DQ issue is detected."*

Sure. Thanks to the improved tech landscape (and AI), we have dramatically improved our ability to detect and report issues at scale and speed. But what we forget is:

We've accelerated detection and notification—but have done little to improve translation and communication.

We still expect business stakeholders to accept the technical status of data quality at face value, reacting and responding to raw data issues without context. And when they don't, we assume they're not invested.

But their pushback is entirely rational. It's the equal and opposite force to how we communicate DQ to them.

Below are some of the most common "reaction forces" from business teams:

- **Language barrier:** Technical teams speak in system fields, schema mismatches, and pipeline failures. The business hears jargon and not value.

- **Misaligned priorities**: A CEO cares about market share and shareholder trust. A supply chain leader cares about on-time delivery. If data quality's role in achieving those outcomes isn't made clear, it feels more like internal noise and not a necessity.

- **Invisible effort:** "Cleaning data" happens behind the scenes. Business users don't see the complexity or effort it takes to make data usable. Without visibility, they often cannot assign value.

- **Complexity fear:** When data feels complicated or overwhelming, business teams retreat to what they know—manual processes, gut feel, or static spreadsheets that feel safer than systems they don't fully trust.

- **Timing mismatch:** Data quality improvement is often a slow, iterative journey. Business leaders operate in fast cycles. If the results don't match their tempo, they usually prefer to disengage.

Each of these reactions is an "opposite force" to your "push" of data quality initiatives. If we want the business to care, participate, and champion better data, we must stop expecting them to adapt to our technical language and start adapting our communication to their world. That means rethinking *not just what we say*...but *how we say it.*

Talk with your business in a language they understand!

Now, let's move on to some standard defaults of data quality that need to change in order to reduce this communication gap.

The juggernaut of data quality dashboards

Let me start with a very familiar scene.

Imagine you've implemented a set of data quality rules on a dataset that supports a key business process. The job runs successfully. Now it's time for the DQ analyst to inform business stakeholders of the results, as part of the issue remediation workflow.

And here comes the most common type of email:

Subject: Weekly Data Quality Monitoring Dashboard Update

Hi [Business Stakeholder Name],

Please find the updated results in our weekly Data Quality Monitoring Dashboard. As part of this week's run, below is an updated summary:

Total number of DQ rules run on DD/MM/YYYY: 237

Number of DQ rules passed: 201

Number of DQ rules failed: 36

Number of DQ issues fixed since last run: 20

Number of DQ issues still open since last run: 49

Most of the rule failures are related to 'Validity' and 'Accuracy' criteria applied to Table ORD_PRD_EXE within our Oracle data store. This suggests potential data entry issues at the source. We have already shared these results with the source development team, who currently have a

backlog. Please advise on the next steps for how we should
proceed.

Thanks,

[DQ Analyst Name]

Weekly Data Quality Monitoring Dashboard

Total DQ Rules Run	Total DQ Rules Passed	Total DQ Rules Failed	DQ Issues Fixed Since Last Run	Total DQ Issues Still Open
237	201	36	20	49

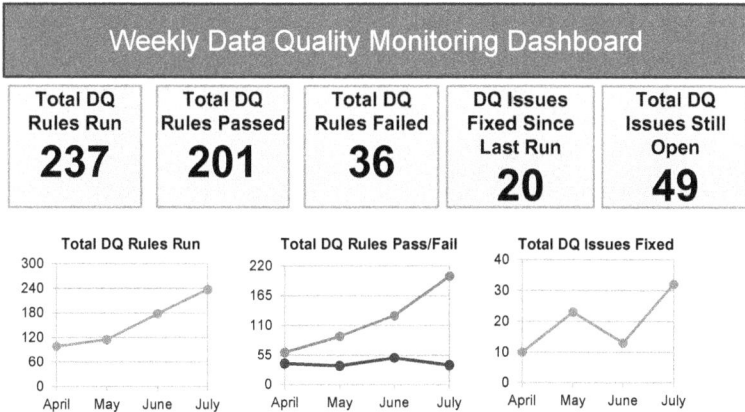

Total DQ Rules Run

Total DQ Rules Pass/Fail

Total DQ Issues Fixed

Now, put yourself in the shoes of a busy business stakeholder as
you read this email and view the attached dashboard. What would
be your instinctive reaction?

For many, the immediate thought is likely, *"Okay... so what? Why
should I, with my packed schedule and strategic priorities, care
about this?"*

And that is the problem.

*For decades, data quality dashboards have remained
largely unchanged.*

Company after company, industry after industry, teams continue to produce technical reports filled with rule counts, pass/fail statistics, and issue backlogs.

For a finance director, a sales leader, a product manager, or a regulatory compliance head looking at this dashboard, their reaction isn't just confusion—it's apathy.

Reiterating it again, it's not that they don't care about data quality. They absolutely do, but only when it's clear how bad data affects what they're accountable for. And this dashboard provides them with absolutely no compelling reason to engage.

What they're asking:

- What does "201 correct results" signify in terms of our actual financial performance or customer satisfaction?
- Do those "36 fatal fails" mean my product performance metrics are wrong?
- Should the supply chain lead be concerned about those "49 unresolved errors"? Are they causing delays, impacting inventory, or frustrating our logistics partners?
- Crucially, which specific business processes, products, or customer segments are being directly affected by these data quality issues?
- Are customers being billed incorrectly?
- Will this impact regulatory reporting?
- Is this issue worth my attention or not?

These are the critical business-centric questions that traditional DQ dashboards almost universally fail to address. As a direct consequence, business stakeholders tune out. The dashboard becomes a mere checkbox in a weekly report; something that might be briefly reviewed or even audited for compliance, but rarely a tool that actively informs their decisions or helps them achieve their core business objectives.

This is the "Law of Action versus Reaction" playing out in real-time. The more technical your dashboard becomes, the more the business pushes back through confusion, disengagement, and mistrust.

It's not a lack of care for data quality itself, but a lack of understanding of its relevance in their language and to their priorities.

Here is how different emotions are manifested by the business when they come across something highly technical in nature:

- **Confusion:** What exactly are these "DQ rules"? What data do they run on? What constitutes a "pass" or "fail"? With no business context, even the most polished report leaves the audience scratching their heads.

- **Disconnection:** Abstract metrics mean little without relevance. *"50 failed rules"*- is that catastrophic? Is it impacting customers? Without tying data issues to real business outcomes, the numbers remain meaningless.

- **Apathy:** If the dashboard doesn't speak to their pain points, priorities, or KPIs, there's no incentive to engage with it. It becomes just another technical report that doesn't inform their decisions or, worse, is ignored entirely.

- **Frustration:** The dashboard reinforces the perception that IT or data teams prioritize internal systems over external impact. Business users often feel like passengers rather than partners in the data quality journey. This reinforces the siloed perception.

Revisit the RevenueValue column example from the last chapter. How would its failure be apparent on a technical dashboard? It wouldn't, until millions were lost in forecasts.

The traditional approach to DQ dashboards, which focuses on rules, counts, and backend metrics, doesn't work for business stakeholders.

Communication only works if it lands where the recipient is.

They don't need technical diagnostics. They need impact narratives.

It's essential to understand how we transition from tech-first DQ dashboards to business-aligned data quality storytelling, with messaging tailored not only for data and engineering teams, but also for decision-makers.

Similar missteps with data quality dimensions

The story of the uninspiring data quality dashboard doesn't end with just rule pass/fail numbers. Lurking beneath those metrics often lies another layer of technical terminology that further alienates business stakeholders: data quality dimensions.

Just as traditional dashboards overwhelm business users with raw counts, so too do the standard data quality dimensions often fail to meet expectations. By definition, a data quality dimension is a recognized term used by data management professionals to describe a feature[2] (characteristic or attribute) of data that can be measured or assessed against defined standards in order to determine the quality of data. In short, that helps quantify "how good" your data is against established standards.

For decades, virtually every book and training material has drilled into data teams the same set of dimensions—completeness, accuracy, timeliness, consistency, validity, uniqueness, and so on. Yet in practice, you'll often see DQ analysts frantically googling to understand the subtle difference between "validity" and "accuracy."

Consequently, every data quality rule implemented is typically tagged with one or more of these common dimensions to quantify the impact of poor data. For instance, if a customer dataset has

---

[2] https://www.sbctc.edu/resources/documents/colleges-staff/commissions-councils/dgc/data-quality-deminsions.pdf.

missing or incorrectly formatted email addresses, the failing rules will likely contribute to a low "Completeness" score for that dataset.

Take our earlier example on the Weekly Data Monitoring Dashboard, if you click through the dashboard details, it dutifully reports something like below:

Scores Per Dimension				
Dimension	Total Rules	Current-Run Failures	Backlog Open Issues	Pass Rate (Score)
Accuracy	70	10	11	70%
Completeness	60	7	10	71.7%
Consistency	50	8	14	56%
Validity	57	11	14	56.1%
Total	237	36	49	

But here lies the same fundamental problem we saw with the overall dashboard: So what? What does that mean to a business user?

- **"Completeness: 71.7%"**—sounds like a puzzle without its picture. Does it mean 30% fewer sales, 30% less revenue, or 30% higher risk of a compliance breach?

- **"Consistency: 56%"**- is that good, bad, or catastrophic? If someone in supply chain or accounting sees that number on Monday morning, do they stop payments or shrug it off?

The truth is, most business leaders don't know or care about these generic labels. For many, these standard data quality dimensions remain abstract and undefined in a way that resonates with their business context. They don't inherently understand the practical implications of a low "Completeness" score on their ability to reach customers or the impact of poor "Accuracy" on the reliability of their sales forecasts.

The data quality teams that diligently assign these dimensions often operate under the assumption that the business inherently understands their meaning and their link to business KPIs. However, this assumption is frequently flawed. In fact, data/IT teams across many organizations have stuck with these same old definitions—never pausing to ask if they make sense in their specific organizational needs and the understanding of their business users.

Sometimes I wonder, "Is there some industry law dictating that every organization *must* adhere to the same canonical set of data quality dimensions?"

Absolutely no, right? If anything, rigidly adhering to those terms only adds confusion.

Then, why can't we define data quality dimensions in a way that directly aligns with the KPIs that matter most to our organization, especially by our analysts, business leaders, and IT partners? And, most importantly, in a language that resonates with and is readily understood by everyone of them?

It's time to go beyond generic dimension matrices and "pass versus fail" indicators that leave business users guessing. In the next section, we'll explore how to design data quality dashboards and reports that tell a story—one that clearly links data conditions to business impact and drives real decision-making.

Why data quality needs its own storytelling

"Data storytelling" has undoubtedly been a buzz phrase at countless industry conferences and forums over the past few years. Virtually everyone in the data world readily acknowledges its importance, urging adoption and emphasizing its transformative power. There are even excellent books and guides on crafting compelling data narratives.

However, in my personal experience, the implementation of data storytelling in organizations often lags significantly behind the widespread acknowledgement of its value. Or, even when adopted, its application is primarily restricted to the reporting and analytics layer, where the focus is more on 'good-looking' visualizing metrics without ever weaving a story around the underlying data. Two main reasons stand out:

1. **No incentive for technical teams:** Data engineers and analysts are often measured on dashboards delivered or lines of code written, not on how a report "feels" to the business. Without a clear reward for translating raw findings into a business narrative, quality conversations stay buried in technical jargon.

2. **Technical mindset:** Even when teams acknowledge data quality issues, they tend to reach for the nearest quick fix like *"Let's validate this field or tune that rule,"* rather than asking, "What does this mean for our CFO, our sales leader, or our compliance officer?" In other words, many technical and data teams don't inherently view data quality from this broader, outcome-driven perspective, remaining narrowly focused on technical solutions rather than translating their efforts into tangible business value.

My aim here is to bridge that very gap. I'm here to show you how to do storytelling specifically for data quality, making it resonate with decision-makers and drive meaningful action.

Let's revisit the "Weekly Data Quality Monitoring Dashboard Update" example we shared earlier in this chapter, which showed raw counts of rules passed and failed and the corresponding dimension table we discussed.

The dashboard example below is not some theoretical construct or random illustration. My teams and I have practically implemented this approach for several clients, and the impact has been genuinely transformative. It demonstrates a clear shift in how data quality is presented, moving it from a technical burden to a clear business enabler.

From failures to business readiness scores

To truly drive engagement, we must perform the essential translation. The "36 failed rules" or "49 open issues" from the technical dashboard aren't just numbers; they are symptoms of underlying data quality problems that directly undermine business objectives. The key is to reframe these symptoms as clear readiness scores and quantifiable impacts that resonate directly with your business leaders, whether it's the CEO, a finance director, or a head of sales.

Below, for our weekly DQ monitoring dashboard, we illustrate how each dimension's technical pass-rate can be converted into concrete business terms, featuring business-friendly percentages for key failure types and a clear line of sight to the KPIs that truly matter.

Weekly Data Quality Monitoring Dashboard

Decision Confidence (Accuracy)	Operational Readiness (Completeness)
70%	**71.7%**
Key Indicators	**Key Indicators**
• Price Discrepancies: 18%	• Missing records: 15%
• Unreconciled Transactions: 12%	• Data dropouts: 13%
Potential Impacts (KPIs)	**Potential Impacts (KPIs)**
• Forecast Accuracy	• Forecast Accuracy
• Revenue Leakage	• Month-End Close Cycle Time
• Order Fulfilment Efficiency	• Expense Reimbursement Turnaround

Cross-System Consistency (Consistency)	Compliance Readiness (Validity + Timeliness)
56%	**56.1%**
Key Indicators	**Key Indicators**
• Mismatches Across Systems: 24%	• SOX controls failing: 19%
• Conflicting or Duplicate Values: 20%	• Audit-Flagged Entries: 25%
Potential Impacts (KPIs)	**Potential Impacts (KPIs)**
• Month-End Close Cycle Time	• Audit Exception Rate
• Customer Net Promoter Score (NPS)	• Time to Compliance

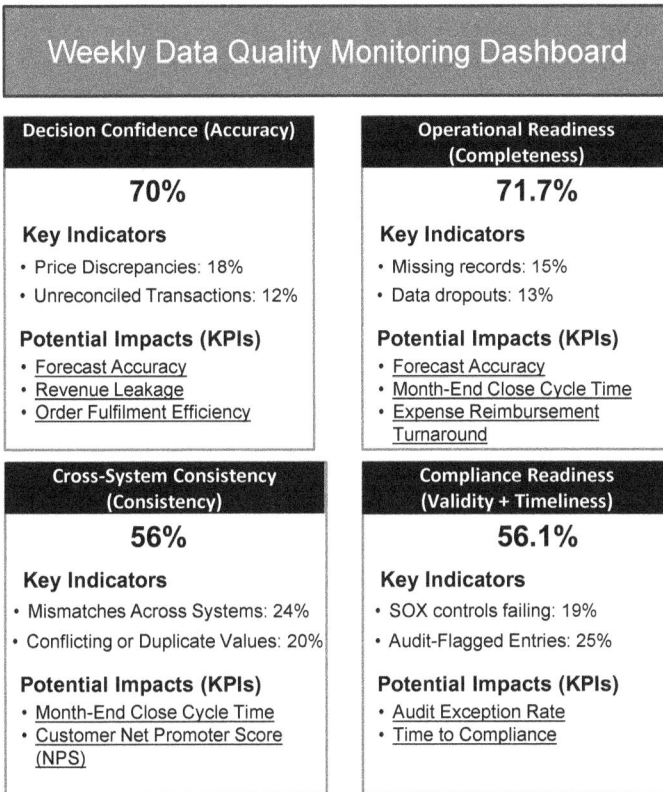

By reframing "completeness," "accuracy," "consistency," and "validity" in the language of business leaders, we shift the conversation from abstract rule counts to actionable, impactful metrics. This kind of explanation can be included within the dashboard itself, or separate document links can be created, which are easy to access and refer to. These can also be made part of your data marketplace or catalog alongside your reporting metadata.

1. Decision confidence (accuracy)

- **Technical score**: 70% (47 of 70 accuracy rules passed; 23 remain unresolved)

- **Business-friendly failure symptoms**:

  - **Price discrepancies: 18%:** Of all invoice and revenue-related records, 18% contain price or cost mismatches flagged by open DQ issues. For example, if 100 customer invoices are issued, roughly 18 have a unit price that do not match the master "price-book."

  - **Unreconciled transactions: 12%:** An additional 12% of transactions remain flagged because invoiced amounts don't match payments or shipments. In practical terms, 12 out of every 100 orders require manual review due to discrepancies in quantity or amount.

Why it matters (Business KPI)

- **Forecast accuracy**: Finance leaders confirmed that price/quantity errors directly skew revenue projections. Currently, at least 30% of invoices contain mispriced or mis-quantified items (18% price + 12% quantity), resulting in a 4–6% variance in quarterly forecasts, which can derail pipeline coverage and lead to either missed sales quotas or excess inventory.

- **Revenue leakage**: The potential for revenue leakage is a critical concern, identified through our discussions with sales operations. Even minor price discrepancies can compound over time. According to business inputs, a single 2% mispricing on a $100,000 order can result in $2,000 of lost or misrecognized revenue. If 18% of our orders are similarly off, those losses can quickly mount, directly eroding profit margins.

- **Order fulfilment efficiency**: Operations teams reported that each unreconciled transaction (12% of orders) causes a manual hold in shipping, adding 1–2 days to fulfilment and driving up logistics costs by 5–7%.

2. Operational readiness (Completeness)

- **Technical score**: 71.7% (43 of 60 completeness rules passed; 17 remain unresolved)

- **Business-friendly failure symptoms**:

  - **Missing records: 15%:** 15 out of every 100 journal entries arrive without a valid General Ledger account code. For instance, 15% of expense reports submitted this month lacked a GL code, forcing manual review. This represents the absence of vital data required for proper financial categorization.

o **Data dropouts: 13%:** 13% of invoices or payment transactions contain a blank or invalid cost-center field. That means 13% of supplier bills are excluded from automated accruals and must be manually tagged.

Why it matters (Business KPI)

- **Month-end close cycle time:** When more than 20% (28% in this case) of finance transactions are incomplete (missing GL codes or cost-center assignments), finance and IT operations teams spend extra days chasing missing fields, pushing the "books closed" date 2–3 days later each month.

- **Financial forecast accuracy:** If more than 10% (15% in this case) of journal entries lack GL codes, automated P&L and balance-sheet rollups can be off by as much as 5–7% until manual correct-and-post cycles finish. That directly impacts forecast versus actual variance analysis and board-level confidence.

- **Expense reimbursement turnaround:** If more than 10% (13% in this case) of expense claims arrive without cost-center tags, the Accounts Payable team can't auto-approve them. That delays employee reimbursements by an average of 3–4 business days, hurting morale and potentially increasing out-of-pocket costs.

3. Cross-system consistency (Consistency)

- **Technical score**: 56% (28 of 50 consistency rules passed; 22 remain unresolved)

- **Business-friendly failure symptoms**:

  o **Mismatches across systems: 24%**: 24% of open issues relate to instances where the same order or customer record in the Sales CRM does not match the corresponding data in the Finance ERP. For example, the CRM shows "Order #1001" = $5,000 shipped to Customer A, but in the ERP, that invoice is recorded as $4,800 or under a different customer code. If you review 100 orders, roughly 24 of them will require manual reconciliation before invoicing and revenue recognition can close properly.

  o **Conflicting or duplicate values: 20%**: An additional 20% issues remain open because key attributes (e.g., "Customer Tier," "Product Category," or "Cost Center") are defined differently in the CRM versus the ERP. For instance, CRM's "Customer A" is labeled "Gold Tier," but in the ERP, "Customer A" appears as "Platinum Tier." Rules executed across a few master records show mismatched reference data, forcing additional manual checks before generating consolidated metrics or profit-and-loss analysis.

Why It Matters (Business KPI)

- **Month-end close cycle time:** When more than 20% (44% in this case) of finance records require manual cross-system reconciliation, finance teams spend an extra 2–3 days every close cycle just fixing mismatches. That means we fail to adhere to board reporting and audit sign-offs SLAs, thus undermining leadership confidence in the finance reports.

- **Net Promoter Score (NPS):** Our marketing and sales leadership consistently raise concerns that when a high number of customers (24% in this case) are misclassified across CRM and billing systems due to inconsistencies, marketing campaigns underdeliver due to incorrect targeting. Customers receive irrelevant offers, which reduces cross-sell uptake and lowers NPS by an estimated 3–4 points (based on past campaign A/B results and direct customer feedback).

4. Compliance readiness (Validity + Timeliness)

- **Technical score:** 56.1% (32 of 57 validity + timeliness rules passed; 25 remain unresolved)

- **Business-friendly failure symptoms**

o **SOX controls failing: 19%:** 11 of 57 total rules remain unresolved because key journal approvals or 'Segregation-of-Duty*' checks are not enforced at the source or the data reflects non-compliance. This means roughly 19% of all financial transactions lack the required SOX control validation.

o **Audit-flagged entries: 25%:** 14 of 57 total rules remain unresolved, where audit teams have flagged missing or incomplete supporting documentation (purchase orders, signatures). That equates to 25% of records currently at risk for external audit exceptions.

Why it matters (Business KPI)

- **Audit exception rate:** With 44% of compliance rules failing, nearly half of all transactions carry an audit exception risk. Historically, as per compliance policy guidelines, a failure rate above 40% correlates with at least two high-severity audit findings per quarter, exposing us to multi-million-dollar fines or restatements.

- **Time to compliance:** Frequently articulated by the Compliance team, resolving all 25 unresolved issues (11 SOX + 14 audit-flagged) demands a manually intensive "fix and revalidate" cycle. Each round of corrections adds days to our annual compliance close, thus delaying

SOX sign-off SLAs and triggering external reviews that prolong our financial close by 3–5 business days.

'Segregation-of-Duty' checks: In the context of SOX (Sarbanes-Oxley) compliance, **"segregation of duties"** means dividing up critical tasks so that no single person can both create and approve a financial transaction. For example, the person who enters a new vendor invoice into the system should not be the same person who authorizes payment for that invoice.

Now, let's re-imagine the same DQ analyst sending the "Weekly Data Quality Monitoring Dashboard Update" email to the business with the above dashboard attached.

Subject: Urgent: Weekly DQ Monitoring Dashboard Risks and Next Steps

To: CFO, VP Finance, Head of Sales Ops, Controller, Head of Compliance

CC: Data Quality Team, IT/Data Engineering, Procurement Lead

Hi Team,

We're pleased to share the latest **Weekly DQ Monitoring Dashboard,** designed to provide clear insights into how data quality impacts our key business operations across various teams. The attached dashboard translates technical data health into actionable business terms, directly influencing our forecast accuracy, operational efficiency, and compliance.

Below is a concise summary of our current data readiness across critical areas, and crucially, what steps we propose next, highlighting how your insights and support are vital in mitigating associated risks and driving continuous improvement.

Current data quality snapshot (Highlights from the dashboard):

- **Decision confidence (Accuracy): 70%**— Our ability to trust data for key decisions needs strengthening.

- **Operational readiness (Completeness): 71.7%**—Gaps in our records are impacting daily efficiency.

- **Cross-system consistency: 56%**—Inconsistent data across systems is leading to manual efforts and delays.

- **Compliance readiness (Validity and Timeliness): 56.1%**—We have significant data integrity issues posing compliance risks.

- **Overall statistics:** 201 data quality rules (out of 237) have passed assigned checks, while 36 have failed to meet required thresholds. Around 20 data issues are open since the last weekly run.

Understanding "What next?" and how you can support mitigation

The dashboard pinpoints specific data quality challenges, creating friction across our operations. The links within the dashboard provide detailed insights into the potential impact on business KPIs. To accelerate improvements, we've curated the email below, which summarizes the challenges and identifies possible next steps. Your active participation is key to success.

Decision confidence (accuracy): Strengthening our foundation for forecasts

The challenge: Our data shows 18% price discrepancies and 12% unreconciled transactions, directly impacting revenue forecasts and sales pipeline analysis.

Our collaborative action: We propose to collectively review the processes around how pricing and order data are entered into our source systems. This includes refining our order entry rules and implementing stricter real-time validation checks. The sales and finance operations team support is critical here: we need their input to clarify master price book rules, review current order entry workflows, and help define new, automated validation points to prevent these errors at the source. We also need a definitive "pricing override" policy for special-price deals to eliminate unauthorized price changes.

Operational readiness (completeness): Streamlining our operations

- **The challenge:** We're seeing 15% of critical financial records missing essential fields and 13% of expected data elements incomplete in flow, impacting month-end close cycle time and reporting accuracy.

- **Our collaborative action:** We need your support to plan this work with Accounting and Accounts Payable teams to enforce "GL code required" validation in the ERP form so that no journal line can post without it. We also need their guidance on which other fields are absolutely critical for smooth processing, and their help in identifying where data "drops out" and testing new workflows that embed completeness. Additionally, we require them to ensure that all new projects and purchase orders include pre-approved cost centers. They can circulate a one-page "Cost Center Cheat Sheet" to every functional team if required.

- **Cross-system consistency: Unifying our data view for faster decisions**

- **The challenge:** We have 24% mismatches across key systems (e.g., CRM versus ERP) and 20% conflicting values for shared attributes, leading to manual reconciliation and delayed reporting.

- **Our collaborative action:** We propose joint "CRM↔ERP Alignment" workshops with key personnel across sales, finance, and other relevant teams to establish clear, unified definitions for shared data elements and implement automated reconciliation processes between critical systems. Your active participation in defining common data definitions and championing their adoption will be vital. If required, you can also pause any campaign builds until the top 24% mismatched customer records are corrected, ensuring a target accuracy for next quarter's major launch.

Compliance readiness (validity and timeliness): Mitigating audit and regulatory risks

- **The challenge:** 19% of financial transactions are failing SOX controls due to data issues, and 25% of records are at risk of being flagged by auditors due to data deficiencies. This creates substantial regulatory and audit risks.

- **Our collaborative action:** We need to jointly review key financial control points and implement stricter, automated validation rules, such as enforcing "Two-Person Journal Approval" in our source systems, to ensure compliance. Our Internal Audit and Legal teams are indispensable here; we need their expert guidance to clarify precise control requirements and prioritize the most impactful validations, thereby reducing audit findings and ensuring timely compliance. We can also conduct a weekly "Audit Triage" call to resolve flagged entries within 48 hours, with one rep from each business unit.

What else do we expect from business leadership?

- **Champion these changes:** Please advise your internal teams and source system leadership to support the adoption of new data-entry validations.

- **Allocate point people:** Each function should name one "DQ Liaison" to join our weekly check-ins.

- **Prioritize high-impact fixes:** Help us prioritize the key issues, like whether we should focus on the top 10 mismatches, missing fields, or audit flags that drive the greatest revenue, cost, or risk exposure.

- **Embed in KPIs:** It would be helpful if you could incorporate "DQ remediation targets" into your department scorecards and performance reviews each quarter. This creates a shared and better

```
    understanding of the state of our data across the
    organization.
```

```
As always, we are here to support you in any way possible.
```

```
Thank you for your prompt attention,
```

<DQ Analyst name>

The extended example email above, detailing the weekly impact of data quality, might appear somewhat extensive. This is mainly because it covers a range of critical issues relevant to multiple business functions. In practice, you would simplify these dashboards and their accompanying communications, tailoring them to specific domains or teams, and restricting details to what is most pertinent to that audience. What really matters here is the *structure and clarity of your messaging.*

This approach focuses on a clear *'call to action'* for the business, delivered in a language they inherently understand. Remember, it's vital to answer the "What's next?" question for business teams. They can't just *guess* solutions by looking at problems on your dashboard.

Imagine a privacy leader, for instance, sees the "Compliance Readiness" metric almost fall to 56%; they immediately grasp the high probability that the company will not meet its regulatory compliance for the upcoming quarter or year. This direct connection to business risk, along with the outlined potential next steps, will readily motivate them to collaborate, not just with data or IT teams, but often with source system owners to collectively fix the issue.

Some of you might argue that calculating these potential impact KPIs is easier said than done, that IT or data teams lack the time or expertise for such intricate analysis, and that their primary focus is automation to save time and money. I agree wholeheartedly. And that, precisely, is why you need metadata as a primary partner for your data quality efforts.

Cataloging your business metadata is critical

All too often, data governance and data quality are viewed as separate disciplines, or even worse, as distinct, siloed efforts. Your metadata exercise, if treated in isolation, or your DQ program, if focused purely on technical validation, will struggle to generate sufficient business value on its own. The real power comes when you connect the two—leveraging rich, comprehensive metadata to drive your data-quality efforts and thereby directly tie those efforts to measurable business outcomes.

To achieve the "Derived Business KPIs" on your dashboards, such as the "Revenue Forecast Accuracy" we showcased in our example, it is critical to explicitly tie your DQ results back to your business elements and metrics. Without systematically cataloging what the data truly means in a business context, data or IT teams will simply lack the necessary visibility to develop or automate these impactful

KPIs, ultimately preventing them from speaking the language of business stakeholders.

Data quality often fails because there is no consensus on definitions, a lack of understanding of the core logic mappings with source fields, and unclear governance. When a CFO asks what "revenue" means and three finance directors give four different answers, that's not a data quality problem. That's an organizational one. And no amount of ETL will fix it.

This fundamental benefit of metadata needs to be communicated to and understood by the business. It may require an initial investment of time and effort in "show and tell" sessions, but the long-term gains in clarity and collaboration are immense.

It is vital to link your data quality rules directly back to your metadata. This connection also enables better categorization of your DQ rules, allowing for accurate management, ownership, and calculation of your business KPIs. Metadata provides the essential business context, data definitions, and lineage information necessary to transform raw data quality findings into actionable business insights. It enables you to:

- **Automate KPI impact calculations:** Instead of manually tracing which reports rely on a given field, a metadata catalog with lineage allows you to identify downstream dashboards and scorecards automatically. For example, "If 10% of **Customer IDs** are incomplete in the CRM, we know that five key revenue reports—Sales Pipeline, ARR

Forecast, Churn Dashboard, Renewals Tracker, and Revenue Monthly Summary will each be off by up to 5%." Once those dependencies are documented in metadata, you can instantly recalculate "Forecast Accuracy Impact" whenever an accuracy rule fails.

- **Enable consistent definitions:** Metadata acts as the central dictionary for your data. When you define a crucial term like" Customer Tier" in metadata as "Values: Gold, Silver, Bronze" (and explicitly linked to corresponding fields in your CRM, ERP, and billing systems), it eliminates all guesswork. Any data steward or IT developer knows exactly how to validate that field across systems without having to force business leaders to translate business jargon or clarify definitions repeatedly. This fosters a shared understanding across the organization. That consistency also ensures that "Tier-based Pricing" rules are applied uniformly, so your DQ checks for "Gold" versus "Silver" don't break because one system uses "Premier" instead.

- **Surface root causes faster:** Metadata captures lineage for critical fields. For example: Order_Amount → Sales.Orders.Amount → Finance.Orders.LineItem_Amount → Revenue_Monthly_Report.Amount. With lineage in place, when a data quality issue arises, you can quickly identify whether a 3% mismatch in "Order_Amount" stems from an ETL transform, a missing currency conversion, or a misconfigured field in the source system. Note, configuring end-to-end lineage is hard and effort-intensive. Hence, focus first on those handful of fields that drive your top KPIs like Invoice_Date, Customer ID, or Revenue_Amount, and then expand gradually.

- **Drive data-driven conversations:** When both business and technical teams share a centralized metadata repository, they see the same picture: Invoice_Date maps to Close_Date on 23 reports, so any gap in that field automatically gives a clear line of sight into which SLAs are at risk due to data issues.

- Instead of arguing "Which report is broken?" everyone focuses on "How do we fix Invoice_Date at the source?" That single shift—common metadata leading to aligned discussions can cut weeks off root-cause analyses and drive collaboration across teams.

By stitching metadata and data quality together, you create a virtuous cycle:

- **Metadata** gives context to DQ failures, enabling automated KPI calculations and consistent definitions. Most importantly, it helps the data teams and functional business teams communicate and align on KPIs with the help of a common point of reference.

- **DQ rules**, in turn, use that metadata to validate precisely the fields that matter most to the business, ensuring every rule can be traced back to a high-impact metric.

Technical DQ dashboards still play a vital role for engineering and data teams. They're indispensable for tracking rule executions, monitoring ingestion pipelines, and pinpointing code-level validation failures. However, those same screens offer little value to business stakeholders. If your goal is to drive true ownership and action, you need a separate, business-focused view, one that translates raw rule counts into the metrics and KPIs that leaders actually care about.

The essence of the Law of Action versus Reaction is simple: every time we push technical jargon onto business stakeholders, we invite equal and opposite resistance. In conclusion, it is critical to remember:

- Business leaders don't need another chart; they need a clear line of sight to their own goals.

- Every rule failure must tie back to a decision, a dollar, or a deadline that matters.

- Your message is only as strong as the language you choose; speaking "business" dissolves the pushback.

In practice, this means creating parallel DQ views. Technical dashboards remain essential for engineers and data stewards; business-focused dashboards are nonnegotiable for executives and functional managers. Together, they ensure that **"action"** always leads to productive **"reactions"**—engagement, ownership, and, ultimately, cleaner, more trusted data.

As Peter Drucker once famously said, *"The most important thing in communication is hearing what isn't said."* In terms of data quality, this means understanding the unspoken questions and unarticulated needs of our business partners, and then crafting our message to address them directly.

Data quality is not just a technical challenge; it is fundamentally a communication challenge.

When we bridge this divide, the resistance dissipates, and the path to truly impactful, business-aligned data quality becomes clear.

Six

Law of DQ Attraction

Newton's fourth law:
All objects with mass attract one another.

Fourth and ultimate law of Data Quality:
Good quality data creates a pull for the business to naturally
revolve around and gravitate toward it.

Business accountability for data quality

Every law we've covered so far was designed to help us fight through resistance, friction, and inertia:

- **Law of Data Inaction** taught us that poor data remains unaddressed unless business sees *why* it matters to daily objectives—otherwise it simply sits there, inert.

- **Law of Unified Data Governance Force** showed us that large data problems (mass) require equally large organizational support (acceleration) to generate meaningful improvement (force).

- **Law of Action versus Reaction** showed us that when data teams act in isolation or with technical tunnel vision, the business reacts with resistance. However, when data quality is communicated in a language everyone understands, adoption becomes a collaborative effort.

Individually, each law helps correct a fundamental imbalance in how organizations approach data quality. But when applied together, something greater emerges:

- You don't have to force people to use good data.
- They start seeking it. Preferring it. Trusting it.
- You've created **gravitational pull**.

This is the *Law of DQ Attraction*: a higher-order outcome that can only emerge when the right inputs are in place. It marks the shift from effortful enforcement to effortless adoption.

When the first three laws are practiced with discipline, the business no longer needs to be pushed toward good data—it pulls itself in. What once required effort becomes a natural gravitation.

Newton's **Law of Universal Gravitation** states:

> *"Every object in the universe attracts every other object with a force proportional to their mass."*

Its elegance lies in its simplicity and its profound impact on our understanding of the universe. We can translate this universal truth directly into the reality of data quality ownership:

> *"Good quality data, by virtue of its inherent trustworthiness and demonstrated value (its 'mass'), creates a powerful pull for the business to naturally revolve around and gravitate toward it."*

Trust me, this is more than a metaphor. It's an operating truth. When your data systems accumulate enough mass, not in bytes, but in business value, they begin to influence behavior. Where previously you fought to get anyone to care about data quality, your business leaders now start asking:

"Is this from a trusted dataset?"
"Why is this dashboard showing only 75% trust?"
"What else can we fix?"

That pull is **earned**, not imposed. It comes only **after** the earlier work of aligning data with purpose, force with ownership, and communication with empathy.

The Law of DQ Attraction is the reward for getting the first three laws right.

What gives data "mass"?

Imagine data not as static files or abstract tables, but as entities possessing **mass**—a quality that determines their gravitational pull on your organization. Just as physical objects draw smaller bodies into their orbit, high-mass data naturally attracts users, processes, and systems. Conversely, poor-quality data carries little to no mass or even negative mass, thus repelling stakeholders and breeding distrust.

When a data asset (whether a source system, an aggregated dataset, a reporting view, or a physical table cluster) accumulates enough mass, it becomes the **default, trusted source**: the bedrock for analysis, the foundation of daily operations, and the first place people turn for answers.

To build that mass and with it, genuine **business gravity,** data must score highly across four key dimensions:

- **Trust as the core element of "mass":** Data that is trusted is inherently more "attractive." This trust isn't built overnight; if data has been consistently accurate, validated, and actionable over time, it gains credibility. When users don't have to second-guess or manually verify data, they naturally gravitate towards it. Stakeholders begin to assume, "If it's in the system, it's right." That trust builds mass.

- **Demonstrated business value:** Mass scales exponentially when data proves its worth in the marketplace. Each time a dataset leads to better decisions, higher revenue, lower costs, better risk control, or improved customer outcomes, its gravitational pull intensifies. When your sales forecast becomes 95% accurate because you've cleaned up customer segment data, or when month-end closes two days faster thanks to complete cost-center tags, stakeholders invest not just effort, but also emotional buy-in. That's the tipping point where data becomes strategic capital.

- **Accessibility and usability:** Even the most trusted, high-value data loses gravity if people can't find it or understand it. Mass must be visible and approachable. Examples include integrated catalogs (a searchable repository where tables, columns, and dashboards are indexed and scored), embedded metadata (definitions, owners, and lineage surfaced within daily tools with no extra login required), and clear interfaces ("Trust Score" badges in CRMs, ERPs, and BI dashboards that signal quality at a glance). When data is just a click away and its meaning is crystal clear, users naturally gravitate toward it rather than resorting to spreadsheets or shadow systems.

- **Relevance:** Mass comes from comprehensiveness and fitness for use. There is no point in boiling the ocean when it comes to data quality. Fixing every possible data issue rarely drives real business value. Most data initiatives stall not because data is unavailable or unclean, but because priorities are unclear. Data that is sharply tuned to the organization's priorities; delivering the right fields, in the right form, at the right time— acquires mass quickly and sustains its pull. That's the 'fit-for-purpose' mindset we discussed in Chapter 4.

Embedding DQ into everyday tasks

If good quality data, by its very 'mass,' naturally attracts the business, then our strategic imperative is clear: we must actively embed data quality controls and feedback mechanisms directly into the tools and processes our teams use every day. These operational or technical" hacks" ensure that trust, completeness, and relevance become baked into every interaction, thus making good data the effortless default. Below are five high-leverage patterns to achieve this:

1. Quality at the point of creation: Integrating DQ checks into core applications

"Shift Left" by applying data-quality rules at the precise moment data is created or updated—inside the very screens your teams live in. When possible, it makes bad data structurally impossible to enter. While "shift left" is often easier said than done and not always feasible for every data source, sustained effort in this direction is crucial.

Example: In your CRM's New Customer form, embed inline validations such as:

- **Email format check:** "Is this address syntactically valid?"
- **Address verification:** "Does this shipping address match the postal database?"
- **Industry taxonomy match:** "Is the selected industry code one of our approved values?"
- **Instant trust feedback:** A dynamic "Trust Score: 75%" badge that updates in real time as fields are corrected.

Effect: Sales reps cannot proceed until the Trust Score meets minimum thresholds. Each correction reinforces good habits, turning data accuracy into an instinctive part of the user journey and building mass at the moment of entry.

2. Enforcing DQ through data contracts

As we discussed in Chapter 2, data contracts formalize agreements between data producers and consumers. To make these contracts truly powerful and embed quality directly into data pipelines, they must include measurable **Service-Level Objectives (SLOs)** for data quality. SLOs are specific, quantifiable targets that define the expected performance of a data product or service, including its quality, thus transforming subjective expectations into concrete, enforceable commitments.

Think of it like the rental agreement between a landlord and a tenant. When a tenant rents a house, the landlord provides a written agreement, not just a verbal understanding, detailing everything present in the house, the conditions of the rental, and how any damages will be handled. The tenant then explicitly agrees to comply with these terms.

Imagine renting a house with no written lease, only a verbal "Sure, just move in and we'll sort it out later." Chaos would ensue:

- What's Included? Is the fridge yours to use? Does the landlord fix the plumbing, or is it on you? Without a written inventory, disputes erupt over every chipped tile or broken faucet.

- Damage Responsibility? Did that scorch mark on the countertop happen before you moved in or after? Without clear clauses, tenants and landlords point fingers, relationships sour, and legal battles loom.

- Payment Terms? What happens if rent is late? Is there a late fee? Can the landlord raise the rent mid-lease? In the absence of defined rules, every payment becomes a negotiation, eroding trust on both sides.

Now transpose that to data:

- **No schema guarantees:** Is 'customer_id' always an integer? Do missing addresses break downstream reports? Without a data contract, every dashboard or ETL job must guess and often fails—inconsistently.

- **Undefined quality expectations:** Must 'order_date' always be present? What's the acceptable error rate for price fields? Without agreed SLOs, producers push half-baked data, and consumers scramble to clean it up.

- **Unclear timeliness:** When will yesterday's transactions arrive in the warehouse? Without freshness clauses, you can't plan your close, your forecasts, or your next campaign reliably.

Just as a written lease creates clear expectations and spares both landlord and tenant from endless disputes, a **data contract** *lays out precisely what data will look like, how often it will arrive, and how "good" it must be.*

When 'honored,' it transforms chaotic, guess-and-check workflows into smooth, predictable collaborations, thus adding enormous "mass" to your data and strengthening its gravitational pull on the business.

I find the concept of data contracts very promising for enhancing data quality in the near future, especially as a means to bridge the communication gap between teams. Of course, it wouldn't solve the challenge completely. Because, unlike a simple landlord-tenant agreement, data quality isn't often a direct agreement solely between the data source (producer) and the final consumer. There can be an infinite number of data transformers in between, and it is inherently complex to manage data "hops" and the SLOs between them, whether manually or automatically through code, some framework, or tools. Plus, even the best contracts assume alignment and similar priorities between multiple teams. Often, the data owners themselves may not be completely aware of the underlying business checks needed (it's an evolving process for many). If the source or data ownership team is swamped with higher-priority work, breaches will occur, and no organization can simply keep on adding unlimited resources to solve data issues for the source teams. We all know and understand this reality.

Still, data contracts offer a powerful starting point. They initiate conversations between producers, transformers, and consumers to agree upfront on schema, quality targets, and freshness expectations and, crucially, to put those agreements in writing. That clarity alone transforms endless back-and-forth into a single source of truth: everyone sort of has an idea on what "good data" means, who's responsible, and how to measure success. There's a long road ahead, but I'm optimistic. Data contracts can be a powerful communication catalyst that finally gets us all orbiting the same trusted datasets.

3. Embed data observability for proactive detection

Another layer of preventive data monitoring that can work hand-in-hand with data contracts is data observability. Data contracts set the expectations between producers and consumers, while data observability makes it possible to continuously verify that those expectations are being met in production. Together, they can form a powerful one–two punch: contracts define the rules, and observability enforces them in real time, often without a single code change.

A common example I often encounter across my projects is a nightly ETL job that runs without errors, but the 'last_update_date' field hasn't been updated in days or weeks. No one has been alerted yet, and downstream reports continue to show "fresh" dashboards, driving decisions that are entirely off from last week's or sometimes last month's reality.

A data observability platform continuously monitors your pipelines for four key signals:

- **Freshness:** Did yesterday's data arrive on schedule?
- **Volume:** Is the record count within ± X% of the rolling 30-day average?

- **Schema Changes:** Has a column been renamed, removed, or had its type altered?
- **Statistical Drift:** Are distributions shifting? (e.g., average order size up/down by > 15%)

By surfacing anomalies as soon as they occur and often triggering automated retries or alerts, observability helps you catch upstream breakages before they ripple into downstream reports and dashboards.

The benefits of data observability directly contribute to increasing data's 'mass' and attraction. These include the ability to create scalable/improved monitoring solutions, streamlined incident management workflows, enhanced operational efficiency, reduced business risk, and a far more immediate time-to-value compared to manual data quality practices. It basically supports the twin aspirations of most modern data teams to catch the issues early before anyone notices and to implement design changes to prevent them from happening again.[3]

However, it's crucial to acknowledge that both data contracts and data observability are still primarily perceived as technical solutions. Their precise impact on complex business outcomes isn't always immediately articulated or quantifiable for business leadership. While incredibly effective at finding corrupted data, detecting data drifts, or ensuring adherence to technical SLOs, they are not the ideal tools for comprehensively testing nuanced

---

[3] https://www.montecarlodata.com/blog-what-is-data-observability/.

business rules or confirming that the data is truly usable and meaningful by end users for complex decisions.

For example, they'll tell you when 5% of orders have missing fields, but most often not whether "all VIP customers were included in this month's sales forecast."

That bridge still requires explicit business input and collaboration. When data engineers are solely responsible for all aspects of data quality, applying data contracts within data operations and leveraging data observability often become the default, fastest options. This leaves a gap in validating the data's ultimate "fitness for purpose" from a pure business logic standpoint.

4. Automate DQ remediation tasks in standard workflows

A common pitfall in data quality strategies is the assumption that simply surfacing bad data will lead to its resolution. In reality, data quality remediation tasks are often missed or deprioritized. To truly add "mass" to data, we must automate the remediation process by integrating it directly into existing workflows.

Please don't assume someone will "get to" fixing bad data by just looking at your alerts or emails. Instead, automate remediation triggers so that corrections are always the next logical step in existing processes.

Example: When a data quality rule fails—for instance, an invoice is submitted without a cost center in the ERP system (a completeness failure). Rather than logging a spreadsheet report and waiting a week for the resolution, create an integrated system that:

- Automatically creates Finance Task #123 in ServiceNow (or your agile DevOps board).
- Assigns it to the department that generated the invoice.
- Requires resolution (selecting the correct cost center) before the next workflow action (such as processing of the invoice) is permitted.

By making remediation a natural, integrated part of existing operational processes, you eliminate siloed resolution of separate "DQ tasks" and empower business users to see that fixing data is simply "the next screen to fill out" or "the next logical step in their workflow," rather than an interruption. Implementing this approach requires proof of concepts between your data quality, IT operations, and business teams. This is definitely achievable.

5. Surface data quality scores at the point of user consumption

Many business stakeholders understandably wouldn't have enough time to log in to separate DQ tools or explore dashboards every time they need insights into the state of data related to their business unit or domain.

The future of data quality lies in making insights effortless and accessible at the precise place and moment they are needed. This is where integrating DQ intelligence into the channels that business users already log in to every morning becomes a powerful mechanism (it's also referred to as 'Active Metadata' by some vendors), basically surfacing information at the very point of user consumption.

Data quality should never be hidden behind engineering pipelines or within DQ tools alone; instead, **broadcast** quality signals at every level, from catalogs to executive dashboards to key applications to communication channels; whichever resonates with the users. This is also an area where AI can offer significant advancements today.

A simple example can be a lightweight chatbot interface into popular collaboration tools like Slack or Microsoft Teams.

A user in a team channel could simply type:

```
@DQBot show revenue_trust_score by region.
```

The bot instantly scans the dashboard metrics and returns:

```
North America: 92%; EMEA: 76% (12% missing pricing data).
```

This allows business users to quickly check data trust snapshots and specific quality metrics without ever leaving their daily chat channels. This instant, low-friction access builds profound attraction over time with a mindset: *"When I'm about to launch a campaign or prepare for a board review, I'll just check @DQBot first to ensure my data is reliable."*

This seamless integration transforms data attraction into an instinctive, daily behavior.

Conclusion

By now, we understand that data quality attraction isn't a lucky accident; it's the inevitable consequence of:

- Tying DQ to real business urgency (Law 1: Inaction)
- Aligning mass-scale problems with unified support (Law 2: Force)
- Speaking business, not technical jargon (Law 3: Action versus Reaction)
- Embedding quality at every touchpoint until data itself becomes the sun around which all teams orbit (Law 4: Attraction).

Follow these in sequence and in discipline and you won't have to cajole or mandate data quality. Instead, you'll find business teams seeking out your trusted datasets, recommending new checks, and celebrating each incremental improvement. They will become naturally, organically, and emotionally invested in DQ success. They will cease to see data quality programs as an imposed technical burden, and instead embrace them as the foundational engine of their success.

As Stephen Covey put it, *"You can't talk your way out of problems you've behaved your way into."* In data quality, we cannot simply talk about its importance; we must behave our way into it, embedding quality into every action, every workflow, until the irresistible pull of good data creates an unbreakable orbit of trust and value.

When you build enough trust, you stop pushing data quality—data quality pulls you.

And that, ultimately, is the mark of a truly data-driven culture.

SEVEN

Data Quality Engagement Mantras

Educate, don't dictate!

There's a fundamental human truth we all recognize yet often struggle to apply in our organizational settings: we inherently resist being commanded or micromanaged. We want to be held accountable for outcomes, yes, but we also crave the autonomy to determine *how* we achieve those outcomes. This deeply ingrained mindset explains why prescriptive directives rarely work, especially when it comes to something as pervasive as data quality management. This is why ownership of data remains a distant dream for many organizations, as we expect stakeholders to accept and react in a particular way, unwittingly creating a barrier to genuine engagement.

But ownership doesn't come from authority. It comes from **belief**. Belief that the work matters. That the data matters. That *their* role in data matters.

To get there, don't dictate. Educate!

The finger-pointing problem

---

*In data quality, we often focus too much on **who's
wrong**, rather than **why it's wrong**.*

The concept of aggregated 'Data Quality Health Scorecards' across business units is gaining momentum within organizations today, but it comes with an inherent problem. You cannot have 10 different unit leaders looking at the dashboard at the same time.

Imagine the CDO team presenting data quality scores for each business team to everyone. Point a finger at a business unit for low data quality scores and you'll almost guarantee one reaction: defensiveness.

It highlights an unspoken "You Lose, We Win" message. Public scorecards may appear to promote transparency, but they are often perceived as shaming. Think about it—who wants to admit their mistakes publicly? No one wants to look bad compared to their teammates or the whole company. No one wants to stand up at the all-hands meeting and admit they're failing. As a result, teams start to hide data issues, game the metrics, or simply disengage.

And eventually, in this game, almost everyone loses. You won't fix data problems by blaming people.

Same story with our source systems

Finger-pointing doesn't stop at business teams. It often *"shifts left"* to the original source systems (ERP, CRM, SAP, etc.), where the common fallback is: "Oh, so we've found bad data? What next? Pass it on to the source team to fix it."

I've heard this line more times than I can count, and honestly, it's unfair to stamp bad data quality solely on the source.

Data quality isn't a problem that begins and ends strictly at the point of creation. Thanks to the hundreds of transformation, aggregation, and integration operations we perform on our data, a data quality issue can creep in at any stage of the data flow, from the initial source system to intermediate data warehouses, expansive data lakes, and final reporting layers. So, while I agree that data engineers and analysts shouldn't be tasked with solely fixing bad data generated upstream, are we truly content with them simply waiting (for weeks or months) for the source to miraculously correct it? Such an approach leads to persistent backlogs and frustrated downstream users.

In my view, there's a deeper challenge here: how we *interact* with source owners. Have your DQ analysts or data stewards ever sat down with those teams to understand how the data is generated or collected? The business context behind it? Their operational limitations? It's unlikely. And it's even more unlikely that they're generating poor data on purpose. For them, that system is operational, driven by day-to-day business needs and processes defined by the business teams. They are not necessarily thinking about the data's analytical downstream usage or its role in a broader data ecosystem.

Most companies have roles like *ERP Application Lead* or *Head of Source System X*. These folks aren't just IT admins; they're senior managers, owners of entire operational workflows, and leaders who genuinely believe they're contributing to business success. They deserve to be treated that way. They deserve a seat at the table when data decisions are made. They deserve to see how their data powers the rest of the business. It's fundamental human nature: they need visibility, and they need to feel their contribution is valued, not just criticized. Too often, they don't get that visibility.

The result? Another blame game, another cycle of passing issues upstream and downstream while business value gets lost in the middle.

Fixing data quality isn't about blaming. It's about ensuring our data enables us to achieve our primary business objectives. Data quality isn't just an extra task that IT handles. It's a key part of how data helps the business succeed.

And it's not just the main data boss (like the CDO's team) who's responsible. Every business leader and stakeholder who interacts with data has a role. Helping your teams understand this shared responsibility is a big part of being a good data leader.

The data literacy universe

Now let's look at the other end of the spectrum—**data literacy programs**.

These are often presented as a new buzzword, and rightly so; building awareness and capability around data is undeniably essential. But here too, there's a common, often overlooked, pitfall.

Many data literacy initiatives, despite good intentions, end up being manifested as:

- A one-time training on some tools or platforms.
- A gamified e-learning module.
- A mandatory slide deck during onboarding.

We must ask ourselves: Is our organization genuinely embracing "data literacy" as a cultural shift, or are we simply checking boxes to say we've done it?

Spending thousands of dollars on building internal training on tools or launching newsletters without a deep understanding of the actual challenges faced by those who work with data daily is, in my opinion, not a fruitful exercise. It certainly doesn't make anyone a truly "data-literate" company.

Teams may learn *about* data, but not what *their* data is doing. They don't see how it affects revenue, risk, or customers. And without that tangible, personal connection, they won't change behavior.

Data literacy must not become a content dump. It must become a culture shift. It should prioritize relevance over rhetoric.

So, how do we transition from finger-pointing and one-size-fits-all training to genuine engagement?

The answer isn't webinars or documents. It's conversations. Context. Empathy. Embedded moments of learning. It's about showing teams the impact of good (and bad) data on their world; not telling them how to behave.

Which brings us to the one thing that works more often than not.

The power of education

Education, done right, is your strongest tool to create lasting DQ engagement.

> *It's not a lecture. It's not a framework. It's an act of translation: from technical language to business reality.*

Below are some key strategies that have proven particularly effective in cultivating this impactful form of education.

Frame data quality as a shared strategy, not an audit

Stop treating data quality like an IT audit checkbox. Instead, position it as **integral** to the organization's top priorities.

- **Recast the narrative:** The first step in effective education is to shift the narrative. Instead of presenting data quality as an auditing function that points out mistakes, position it as an intrinsic part of the business's overarching strategy. The message should be clear: "Improving data quality isn't about correcting errors for their own sake; it's about accelerating our customer satisfaction scores, shaving days off the financial close, and driving higher ROI on every marketing dollar."

- **Speak their language:** Remember our action versus reaction law of data quality? Show business leaders precisely how cleaner, more reliable data measurably accelerates *their* key metrics, whether it's enhancing customer satisfaction, drastically reducing time to close financial periods, or boosting the Return on Investment (ROI) of marketing campaigns. For instance, a 5% increase in data completeness can translate into a 3% higher quarterly revenue.

- **Elevate the conversation:** When leaders see data quality as a lever for growth rather than an IT deliverable, engagement becomes a strategic choice, not a technical burden.

Cultivate private, constructive dialogues

Public scoreboards and generalized critiques often trigger defensiveness. A far more effective educational approach is to engage in private, constructive dialogues.

- **Collaborate to find solutions, not blame, in one another:** Organize one-on-one or small-group sessions with relevant business leaders and their teams. These are not blame sessions; they are collaborative problem-solving opportunities. Come prepared with concrete, anonymized examples of how poor data specifically impacted *their* profit & loss (P&L), *their* project deadlines, or *their* customer relationships.

- **Listen first:** Ask leaders where they feel the most friction, such as delayed reports, lost deals, or compliance headaches.

- **Map solutions to pain:** Show, step by step, how targeted DQ improvements can eliminate their specific headaches, making the business case unmistakable.

- **Approach with empathy:** Most importantly, approach these conversations with genuine empathy, demonstrating a clear path from good data health to their personal and team success.

Improve collaboration with source system owners

Blaming ERP or CRM teams for "bad data" is a dead end. Instead, build a **partnership**:

- **Establish a clear ownership matrix:** Define which team owns each data domain, and how responsibilities will be shared when issues arise.

- **Embed root-cause analysis and resolution into process:** When a DQ rule fails downstream, the resulting dashboard automatically classifies the issues into relevant categories and routes the issue to the right source-system owner, accompanied by proposed causes, suggestions, and corrective steps documented by data stewards. This single step demonstrates that you are not playing the blame game, but instead want to solve issues with the source system stakeholders collaboratively.

- **Leverage data governance as the glue:** The DG team (remember our unified force) convenes source and downstream stakeholders, navigates best practices, and provides access to the quality tools, metadata catalog, playbooks, and relevant documentation to keep everyone aligned.

By treating source-system leads as strategic partners, inviting them to planning sessions, sharing dashboards, and recognizing their contributions, you transform "them versus us" into **"all of us together."**

Remember, no team creates bad data on purpose!

Challenge the self-service fantasy

One of the biggest myths in the modern data management ecosystem is that *self-service* alone will fix everything. Software vendors promise us a future where business users can independently define data quality rules, maintain dashboards, and resolve data issues without requiring a central team. Reality, however, is very different.

For most organizations, true self-service is a long-term destination, **not a starting point**. We can't expect busy sales directors, finance managers, operations leads, or domain owners to magically understand profiling, rule writing, or root cause workflows just because we gave them a shiny new tool.

If you roll out a DQ strategy or tool and expect business users to run with it alone, you'll likely see minimal adoption and superficial fixes, of course, followed by frustration. They don't know where to start. They fear breaking something. And they certainly don't want to be blamed if the rules they configure go wrong. Yes, cultural enablement, training, and literacy take time.

That's why the real work is *hand-holding*. At least for the first couple of years, data and IT teams must guide the business stakeholders step-by-step:

- Show them what good DQ actually looks like in their day-to-day work.
- Explain how to interpret profiling results.
- Help them prioritize which rules matter most.
- Partner on defining rules together—translating business logic into data checks that make sense.
- Keep iterating side-by-side until the process feels intuitive.

Self-service is powerful *when teams are ready*. But that readiness is built on trust, coaching, and co-ownership. If you jump straight to federation without this foundation, you're just pushing the problem further out, creating confusion instead of empowerment.

So, don't assume ownership will magically happen. *Grow* it, deliberately, with education at every step. One day, those business teams will truly self-serve, but only because you didn't abandon them at the start.

Embed data literacy into daily routines

Generic e-learning modules, while scalable, often fail to create lasting behavioral change. Data literacy isn't easy or a one-size-fits-all setup. It needs significant efforts and articulation across diverse groups of stakeholders within our organizations.

True data literacy must be seamlessly integrated into the daily fabric of an organization. This means creating ubiquitous "DQ moments" that are brief, impactful, and contextual learning opportunities that become part of existing routines, not an extra chore.

Of course, the macro-level initiatives like hands-on training, cultural awareness, and user enablement-based learning should continue in parallel.

However, we can also consider embedding these micro-learning opportunities:

- A concise, 5-minute 'Data Quality Demo' during the weekly team stand-up, focusing on one specific, relevant data element.
- A quick "Data Clinic" drop-in session immediately following the monthly leadership review, where teams can bring specific data challenges for on-the-spot guidance.
- Making basic data cleanliness checks an integrated part of an existing workflow, such as prompting for data validation during an approval process or offering intelligent autofill suggestions in data entry forms.
- Quick reference guides and trust-score badges are woven directly into the applications people use every day.

By doing such micro-level activities, we ensure that understanding and action become reflexive. This approach eliminates the feeling of being "trained" and instead fosters a continuous learning environment where data quality is a natural, invaluable part of everyone's job.

Data literacy is more of a process-driven initiative; technology or tools act as an enabler within it. I believe data literacy should be more people-intensive than technology-driven. This is why soft skills matter more here than technical ones.

> *The most effective data governance professionals aren't the loudest in the room; they're the most trusted.*

Eventually, proper education in data quality is about empowerment over instruction. Context over control. Such approaches respect the autonomy of business leaders while providing them with the necessary insights to make data quality a personal priority.

Are older folks really reluctant to adopt data quality? How true is this?

One of the most bizarre inputs I have heard from data quality skeptics is "No matter what you do to convey data quality benefits or educate them, our more tenured employees just won't adopt data quality. They are way too resistant to change what's been working well for years."

In my experience, that belief is more of a myth than a reality. I've been mentored by some of the brightest, most seasoned business leaders who fully grasp the value of a clean, reliable data estate. Yes, long-standing professionals can be resistant, but not to the *idea* of better data. They're wary of *sudden*, disruptive change.

We can all agree that change is inherently hard, especially when it involves adopting new processes and technologies that disrupt established ways of working.

As Simon Sinek puts it, *"People don't fear change, they fear sudden change."* Domain or business experts have often spent years meticulously building their existing systems, processes, and methodologies. They logically fear that any new data quality processes might negatively impact their hard-won efficiencies, involve costly re-training for their personnel, or even suggest that their long-standing efforts were somehow flawed. And when you have spent years building and perfecting something, a sudden, imposed change is naturally met with reluctance.

It's important not to frame data quality initiatives in a way that implies they've been doing something "wrong." Instead, position DQ as an evolution, a next step to build upon their existing foundations. To move beyond blanket resistance, data quality teams should combine **People**, **Process**, **Technology**, and **Data Literacy** into a cohesive change-management strategy:

- **People are at the heart of change:** It's simply unfair to expect individuals who have spent years perfecting a particular way of working to pivot overnight. Change must be embraced in gradual stages, becoming a cultural shift that is digested one bite at a time. This requires patience, understanding, and consistent reinforcement.

- **Processes to guide the evolution:** Rome wasn't built in a day, and neither is successful data quality. The journey unfolds in stages. The key is to understand the unique challenges and operational rhythms of each specific business or domain team. Simultaneously, it's about empowering your central data governance team to provide consistent guidance. The goal is to present a united front: a centralized data governance team that provides DQ frameworks, processes, and tools that are thoughtfully customized for the entire organization. It's about laying the groundwork and providing clear, navigable pathways before asking for a monumental leap. We discussed earlier the effectiveness of embedding central DQ analysts or experts within domain teams on a project basis. These analysts can demonstrate how these changes directly benefit the specific team, guiding them through the transition with hands-on support. When teams see tangible advantages directly relevant to their work, they'll more eagerly embrace the new way.

- **Technology as the silent enabler:** Technology isn't merely a tool; it's a powerful enabler that can subtly drive change. The right set of data catalog and quality tools can visually demonstrate the value of DG and DQ initiatives in a way that resonates with business users. By streamlining and templating key data activities, technology becomes a driving force for efficiency within teams, making the new way easier than the old.

- **Data literacy:** Beyond people, process, and technology, data literacy, which we've discussed earlier in this chapter, stands as the critical fourth pillar. All these enablers require real conversations, collaborative workshops, continuous engagement, and yes, sometimes even a touch of fun, to ignite a positive outlook towards data governance and quality. Relying solely on virtual enablement won't suffice for achieving deep-seated behavioral shifts.

The objective is clear: to shift the narrative around data quality from being a "good-to-have" to an undeniable "must-have" for every individual's success.

We aim to encourage genuine participation, rather than coercion.

Get everyone in a room!

You'll often witness a common situation within organizations. Multiple teams, sometimes unknowingly, are working on their own distinct data-related use cases. They seek separate yearly budgets, hire individual specialists or consultants, and invest in disparate tools.

Whether it's the recent surge in Generative AI initiatives or your traditional ERP cleanup or operational reporting projects, on the surface, they may appear distinct. Still, underneath, they all grapple with the same core challenges: data collection, cleansing, storage, and reporting. Everyone touches data, so everyone owns part of the data-quality burden. Yet when teams work in isolation, they duplicate effort, waste resources, and miss the bigger picture.

To truly address these challenges at their root and foster efficiency over duplication, stakeholders across these teams need to come together directly and collaboratively. While virtual meetings are sufficient for follow-ups and routine check-ins and yes, we understand the real-world restrictions around travel, sustainability efforts, and busy calendars. Still, if you genuinely value the criticality of high-quality data within your organization and aspire to uncover what's most bothering the business when it comes to data, you need to bring everyone together **in a room.**

The Market Research Syndrome

Another common approach many companies adopt to understand their internal data landscape is to deploy broad surveys and questionnaires, aiming to map who is working on what data activities, what they need, and where the pain points lie. But think for a moment: When was the last time you honestly and enthusiastically answered a survey of 100+ questions about your data work, only to realize most of them had little relevance to what you *actually* do, or that a multiple-choice answer couldn't possibly capture your nuanced daily struggles?

Similarly, some companies rely heavily on industry research guides to inform their data strategy or dictate which tools or technologies to license. Yes, research guides are handy, primarily for understanding macro trends, emerging technologies, and the broad direction of the industry. However, what I've also been observing lately is that some executives are enforcing these reports blindly onto their teams without first thoroughly understanding their own organization's unique context, specific data ecosystem, and inherent challenges.

If you genuinely want to solve your data issues at the root, **talk to your 'People.'** Their lived experiences, accumulated knowledge, and day-to-day frustrations are invaluable. Pair that authentic internal insight with market research, and you'll be far closer to building effective, tailored data solutions that truly resonate and deliver.

So, what are some practical solutions to these concerns?

Build communities of practice, from bottom to top

Beyond the limitations of surveys and the dangers of blind reliance on external reports, another fundamental challenge exists within traditional "data governance committees" or "data governance councils." There are so many such committees, forums, and councils we have collectively created over the years! And how many of your executives regularly attend these meetings? I think we all know the answer here.

Often, these forums and their discussions are limited to senior leaders across business units, with little to no direct involvement from the personnel who work directly with the data, such as data stewards, data analysts, governance or quality consultants, or even data engineers. The fact is, nobody truly understands the daily problems, the small details, and the clever solutions in data projects better than the people who are *doing the work*. These are the individuals who face challenges, try various solutions, and find ways to accomplish their goals.

The issues these leaders discuss in their high-level virtual council meetings are mostly superficial or merely derived from their internal, perhaps filtered, conversations with their direct reports. Is that truly helpful for tackling complex, granular data quality issues? Shouldn't the very people who work day in and day out with the data get a direct opportunity to present their ground-level challenges and propose practical solutions? As a result, the analysts, the engineers, the governance folks (those in the lower "pecking order"), often feel unheard or ignored. They need their own spaces to discuss, collaborate, and identify solutions.

The ideal structure, therefore, should foster communities of practice that cascade from the bottom to the top: starting with active communities for data analysts, data engineers, and data stewards. Representatives from these active communities should then get a seat, or at least a regular voice, in the data governance councils. This ensures that real-world data challenges and opportunities inform the discussions at higher levels.

When stakeholders at all levels feel their voices are heard, their concerns are genuinely addressed, and their contributions are valued, these governance forums move from being a bureaucratic exercise to a powerful, value-driving force for the business. Remember, data governance is, at its heart, a **people-first process.** Technology can support and automate, but the fundamental transformation begins when people collaborate with clarity and shared goals.

Thus, the next time you establish a governance committee, begin with the people, not the processes. This is how governance forums can evolve from silent, siloed discussions into being true enablers of business success.

The **Data Quality Engagement Pyramid** can follow targeted versions of the structure below for your organization:

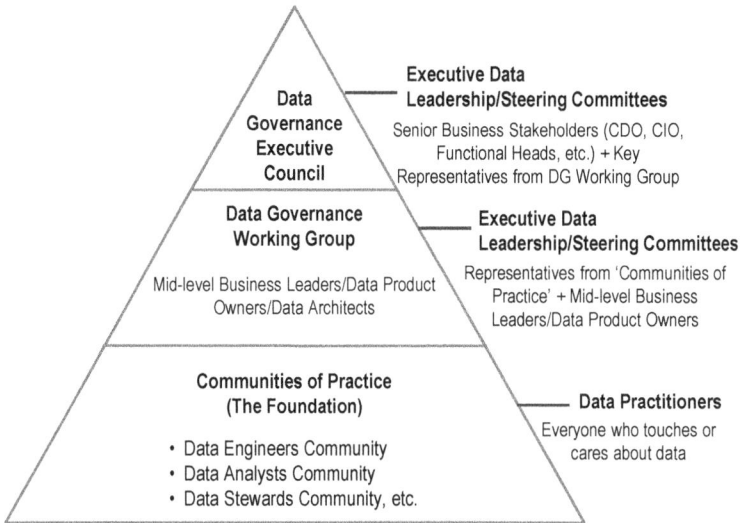

Adopt a DQ war room strategy

Complex data problems often require a level of focused teamwork that regular meetings cannot provide. Let me give you an example from the consulting industry. As part of the typical sales process, companies issue a "Request for Proposal" (RFP) that outlines their challenges and requests solutions. Many of these RFPs are critical, representing millions of dollars, extreme complexity, or vital client relationships, and require intense brainstorming. A common strategy adopted by consultants is a "War Room" approach: consultants co-locate, often getting "locked" in a conference room for days (sometimes weeks) to forge a strong, cohesive solution proposal that helps carefully draft the nuances of clients' problems, their processes, and prepare a roadmap to action it in a step-by-step approach.

I think data quality deserves the same urgency. Data quality is a complex challenge for many organizations, making dedicated, often co-located, collaboration essential. Could we achieve the same breakthrough virtually for complex DQ problems? Often, the answer is no. This is because simply gathering stakeholders to discuss complex challenges isn't enough.

A truly productive forum requires more than just meetings; it needs:

- Focused deep dives and collaboration strategies
- Rapid iteration on problems and solutions
- Clear understanding of roles and precise assignment of responsibilities, and
- An aligned purpose.

The first step to success in tackling these complex DQ challenges lies in understanding who your data producers, data transformers, and data consumers are, and then physically getting them into a common location for focused work. Each of these stakeholders plays a unique and critical role, and aligning their perspectives in real-time is paramount. Within such a "DQ War Room" strategy:

- **Identify the players:** Begin by clearly mapping out your data ecosystem. Who creates the data at its source? Who transforms or manages it along its journey? Who uses it to make crucial decisions?

- **Learn more about them as 'humans':** Begin with small introductions, understand who these people are, their background, and cultures. Start with engaging ice-breaker sessions.

- **Understand their challenges and expectations:** Facilitate direct, in-depth discussions. What specific pain points do they face with data in their daily roles? What outcomes do they care about most?

- **Align on purpose:** Define clear, shared objectives for the collaboration that resonate with everyone. This moves the discussion beyond general problems to focused, collective solutions. Use techniques such as fishbowl interviews, live mapping, and sticky-note sessions to capture pain points and identify quick wins.

- **Assign roles and responsibilities:** Clarify who will lead root-cause analysis, rule-implementation, DQ monitoring, issue remediation, and change-management communications.

- **Co-create KPIs and ownership models:** People own what they design. Involve business leaders directly in defining the data elements that matter most to our objectives, determining how will we measure success (whether it's a specific completeness score threshold or a quantifiable reduction in manual reconciliation time), and uncovering everyone's preferred way to monitor progress (whether it's a specific dashboard, a recurring report, or even a direct Slack alert). War rooms transform abstract mandates into concrete action plans, and they foster the personal connections necessary for ongoing collaboration. This collaborative design fosters genuine buy-in. When teams actively set their own data quality targets, they naturally take pride and ownership in achieving them. True engagement is achieved when stakeholders genuinely feel invested in the solution, rather than merely being subjected to it. Empower them by giving them significant freedom in how they monitor and improve those metrics, rather than dictating the methods. The emphasis should be on holding them accountable for progress against "jointly established goals," transforming compliance into commitment.

- **Create a "data translator" role:** As we have consistently discussed, the importance of translating data quality concepts into a language understood by everyone cannot be overstated. For these intensive "war room" workshops, assigning a dedicated **Data Translator** role can be incredibly effective. I was fortunate and passionate about playing such roles in most of my client engagements. Many successful companies have implemented this by assigning individuals to work closely with specific business units.

To bridge the gap between technical teams and business users, and maximize the productivity of these collaborative forums, designate a Data Translator, a liaison who:

- Facilitates war-room discussions, ensuring everyone speaks a common language.
- Translates DQ metrics into business KPIs (cost savings, efficiency gains, compliance scores).
- Educates both sides on constraints and priorities, fostering mutual empathy.

In a nutshell, when stakeholders see that their voices shape the solution and when they co-own both the problem and the plan, data quality stops being a siloed chore and becomes a unifying force for business success. Hence, next time you want to draft a data quality plan, first get everyone in a room!

Catch the no. 2's in the value chain!

Modern data landscapes today are intricate, and data is just everywhere, fueling initiatives across all business departments within our organizations. When it comes to improving data quality across the organization, many data and IT teams instinctively aim straight for the top of the business hierarchy, such as the head of the business unit, a senior leader, or a key decision-maker. While top leaders set big plans, the real day-to-day details about how business processes work and what the data truly means often come from people who are just below the very top. Getting these key people involved is not just a good idea; it's a must for making your data processes strong and reliable.

The "Special Someone" Syndrome

One of the biggest hidden risks in any organization's data quality ecosystem is the "Special Someone" syndrome. You know exactly who this is: the one person who knows *where* the real numbers live, *which* tables are up to date, *what* is the right definition for a field, *how* that cryptic field is calculated, or *why* a certain data quality rule was added three years ago but never appropriately documented.

Every business department has its "special someone"—the person that every business leader calls when the numbers look off, when the report breaks, when an auditor asks a tough question, or whenever a data question arises. For years, this has worked fine, until it doesn't.

I've seen firsthand how entire million-dollar reporting pipelines can hinge on just one person's knowledge. Remember the example I mentioned earlier about the $1 billion in phantom sales that appeared during the Christmas week? That mess happened simply because the "special someone" who knew which seasonal adjustment rule to toggle was on holiday. The system worked perfectly until it relied on a human brain that wasn't there.

When that person leaves the company, takes another role, or goes offline for a week, the organization is left scrambling, sending urgent emails, pulling late-night fixes, or re-checking dashboards line by line.

This isn't just inefficient; it's a massive business risk hiding in plain sight.

Building the foundations of data quality with no. 2's

One of the biggest hidden risks in data quality programs is that critical knowledge often lives only in a few people's heads. Trust me, the "special someones" aren't intentionally hoarding data information or hiding critical details. It's often because they've never been empowered to see the big picture or the end-to-end journey and impact of the data they manage. Just as we discussed earlier, similar to how data engineers or developers often work in technical silos, unaware of the broader business perspective, these "business side experts" might be equally unaware of the data or IT team's overall vision or processes. At its heart, it's all about people; our perspective changes depending on which "side" of the data journey they're on. To bridge this gap effectively, it's crucial to genuinely hear them, understand their context, and empower them to connect the dots.

The antidote to the "Special Someone" syndrome isn't to discourage individual expertise, but to broaden its reach and embed it within your data quality strategy. The key lies in identifying, engaging, and empowering the "special someone," or as I call them, the "number twos" in your data value chain.

Who are these "number twos"? They are usually not the top bosses, but they are the analysts who build critical dashboards, the operational managers who verify nightly reports, the subject-matter experts who know precisely how a field is calculated. They work at the granular level where business processes are defined, data is created, consumed, and often where its quality breaks down. Senior leaders trust them for detailed insights; IT teams respect their hands-on experience. Basically, they are the experts within their domain; the go-to person for most. When these experts are fully engaged, they can translate lofty data quality goals into practical steps that fit daily routines.

You might be thinking: "Aren't these just our business data owners or business data stewards?" In some organizations, those titles are indeed meant for this purpose—provided those role-holders have genuine end-to-end domain expertise.

Unfortunately, in many companies, those roles become nominal "delegates" with limited authority or perspective. Our goal is to evolve those positions (and similar ones) into true no. 2's: empowered individuals who bridge strategy and execution, fully versed in both business process and data. If your organization has such individuals assigned to the right roles, you already have a good head start to build upon.

How to get them involved smartly:

- **Actively identify and make them feel special:** Don't wait for a crisis to discover these invaluable individuals. Actively seek them out and recognize their unique blend of operational expertise and data understanding. Make them feel special because they truly are publicly acknowledged. Bring them into data quality meetings (not just IT-only sessions) and give them early access to important dashboards, data quality scorecards, or tools. This formal recognition builds on their informal influence.

- **Create safe spaces for them to share:** Beyond inviting them to meetings, actively build environments where they feel comfortable sharing their detailed knowledge and frustrations. This means:

  o Organizing regular "data huddles" or small workshops where they can speak openly about specific data pain points and offer insights without fear.

- o Making it absolutely clear that the goal isn't to assign blame, but to achieve improvement collaboratively.

- **Include them to streamline DQ processes:** Involve these experts directly in defining data quality rules, designing monitoring dashboards, and streamlining remediation processes. Their insights will ensure DQ initiatives are not only technically sound but also pragmatic, contextually relevant, and easily integrated into daily operations. They can pinpoint the precise points where data errors can get introduced and suggest the most effective fixes that won't disrupt critical workflows.

  - o *Example:* Instead of a data team guessing which fields are critical for customer segmentation, involve a senior marketing analyst who builds the segments daily. They can articulate the exact data fields that, if missing or inaccurate, would render a campaign useless, allowing DQ efforts to be precisely targeted.

- **Turn their local knowledge into institutional knowledge:** The insights from these experts are priceless. Make a concerted effort to document the data quality rules and nuances they apply informally in their daily work.

> o   Automate these rules where possible within systems, or at the very least, standardize them in shared data glossaries, dictionaries, and metadata tools. This transforms critical, undocumented local knowledge into resilient, accessible institutional knowledge, making the organization less vulnerable.

- **Leverage them as communication bridges:** Ensure they are part of your data governance councils or committees. These experts speak both "business" and "data." They can translate technical challenges into business impacts for senior leaders and convey leadership priorities back to operational teams. This two-way communication turns committee discussions into concrete, actionable problem-solving. This helps ensure that data quality discussions move beyond superficial committee meetings to concrete, actionable problem-solving.

- **Reward and recognize their contribution:** Beyond formalizing their role, make data quality part of performance conversations. Celebrate their success in town halls or internal newsletters, and consider small awards or tokens of appreciation. Over time, this actively builds a culture where people view sharing knowledge and contributing to data quality as valuable, rather than threatening, and fosters a sense of collective ownership.

By proactively identifying, valuing, and involving these no. 2's, you tap into a wealth of operational insight, remove hidden bottlenecks, and ensure that data quality initiatives remain grounded in real-world practice. This approach transforms fragile, person-dependent processes into robust, shared capabilities, which ultimately is one of the critical pillars of a successful data quality management program.

The last point on reward and recognition needs more attention and discussion.

Actively seek and act on feedback

If Newton's third law teaches us that every action has an equal and opposite reaction, then in data quality, the reverse is also true. Every action you take to involve stakeholders must generate a positive reaction, resulting in more ideas, deeper ownership, and genuine enthusiasm. Without continuous feedback, recognition, and incentives, even the most effective data quality programs will lose momentum. This mantra focuses on understanding the human element behind sustained data quality and is built on the three pillars of feedback, recognition, and incentives, woven together into a continuous cycle that transforms one-time wins into a lasting culture of quality.

Early in my career, I led a data quality project for a large retailer whose product teams struggled with noisy order data. One day, a finance analyst (outside our usual circle) suggested a tweak to the online ordering system. That single idea cut source-data errors by over 60% overnight. Apart from the power of listening, this incident taught me two profound lessons:

- No single data team can match the collective insight of domain experts.
- Opening feedback channels transforms isolated fixes into organization-wide improvements.

When you genuinely ask for feedback, you demonstrate that stakeholder input profoundly matters. This act of listening cultivates deep trust and encourages broader, more consistent participation. Without structured, accessible feedback channels, business users can easily feel like data quality is a robotic activity, merely tasked with chores (like correcting errors) but never truly heard when they raise important issues or innovative ideas.

Practical steps to cultivate feedback:

- **Establish an open suggestion registry:** Move beyond informal channels or one-off surveys. Maintain a shared digital document or a dedicated portal where anyone can easily propose data quality improvements, comment on others' ideas, and collectively up-vote the highest-value suggestions. This transparency fosters a sense of collective ownership and innovation. This registry can be your data catalog or marketplace.

- **Host regular "data quality voice" sessions:** Organize short, focused sessions or "huddles" such as monthly open forums or office hours where "number twos" and other domain experts can surface pain points, share quick wins, and even collaboratively co-design small experiments or solutions in real time, without a rigid agenda.

- **Implement rapid triage and response:** Listening is only half the battle; acting on feedback closes the loop and builds trust. Assign a small, dedicated team to review all submitted feedback within 48 hours. Even if a suggestion is deferred, a prompt and transparent acknowledgment, explaining *why* (e.g., "not in this quarter's scope," "resource constraints"), shows you're truly listening and that their input is valued. Maintain a living, publicly-accessible data quality roadmap or backlog where suggestions are tracked, along with their status (accepted, in progress, deferred) and the reasons for decisions.

Outcome: Transparent feedback loops actively break down organizational silos, spark powerful cross-team collaboration, and ensure that small yet profoundly impactful ideas never get lost in the noise, leading to continuous improvement.

Recognize contributions publicly

This part of the mantra focuses on cultivating an internal culture of appreciation and participation among contributors. Celebrating contributions transforms isolated successes into shared victories. When people see their efforts are genuinely acknowledged and their impact highlighted, it sends a clear message: data quality genuinely matters here, and *their* contribution to it is valued. This amplification encourages others to step forward with their own ideas and fixes.

Effective recognition strategies:

- **Spotlight champions:** Go beyond simple mention emails. Feature standout contributors or teams in town-hall shout-outs, internal newsletters, or create a rotating

"DQ Champion" bulletin board. Highlight the specific person or team who had the most impactful insight or implemented a critical fix each quarter, explaining the business value of their contribution.

- **Involve them in leadership forums:** Elevate key contributors beyond their immediate teams. Invite them to co-present case studies in governance councils or lead workshops on specific successes in data quality. This provides them with visibility, validates their expertise, and inspires others.

- **Offer tangible tokens of appreciation:** While grand gestures are nice, even small things can leave a big impression. A personalized, handwritten note from a Chief Data Officer or a senior business leader, branded merchandise, or a framed certificate of appreciation for a significant improvement in data quality can make a world of difference in individual motivation. I have personally experienced it!

Outcome: Public recognition amplifies engagement, encouraging others to step forward with their own ideas and fixes.

Incentivize ownership with aligned rewards

At its core, data quality often suffers from a **Principal-Agent Problem**. This economic concept explains why data quality initiatives frequently fall short. Simply put: if you are the Principal, the one who directly benefits from or is harmed by an outcome, you care intensely and ensure quality. But if you are merely the "Agent," doing something on someone else's behalf, you often optimize for your convenience or efficiency rather than for the true, long-term value of the asset.

In data quality, IT or data teams often act as Agents, tasked with fixing issues because the business (the Principal) expects them to. Their incentive might be to close tickets quickly, rather than optimizing the data's long-term business value. The key to solving this is to tie performance metrics and rewards directly to data quality outcomes, effectively making everyone a Principal. If data producers, business teams, and consumers view data quality as their responsibility, rather than just IT's, organizations will naturally improve data quality. This shift transforms data quality decisions from fear-based ones (e.g., "If we don't fix this, something bad will happen") to desire-based ones ("We desire to achieve greater good for the company with the help of the amazing data we possess!").

Some of the effective incentive ideas in my experience are:

- **Tie rewards to business-aligned KPIs:** The most powerful incentives are those directly linked to clear, measurable business outcomes affected by data quality. For example, offer team rewards when data quality improvements lead to a "50% reduction in billing disputes" or "98% accuracy in on-time delivery metrics." This ensures participants see how their data quality efforts feed back into the success metrics they genuinely care about.

- **Offer skill-building rewards:** Invest in the development of those who champion data quality. Every incentive doesn't have to be monetary in nature. People care about their personal and career goals with equal importance. Offer them fast-track training on advanced tools to excel in their data knowledge, and passes to industry conferences and webinars. Most people love networking and improving their professional connections, and mentorship sessions with senior leaders for individuals driving the biggest DQ improvements. This links data quality contributions to career growth.

- **Grant resource allocations:** Reward teams that demonstrate sustained impact on data quality with small project or POC budgets and dedicated headcount, let them explore new ideas to refine internal data processes further and drive business value. This empowers them to take on further initiatives and reinforces that data quality improvements are valued with tangible support.

When data producers, transformers, and consumers see direct monetary or non-monetary benefits from high-quality data, they shift from reactive fixers to proactive owners.

Invest in PR!

While it's fundamentally important to reward and recognize the individuals diligently interacting with and improving data at all levels, it is equally, if not more critical, to recognize and champion the collective effort driving the entire data quality program within your organization. Whether it's the Chief Data Officer (CDO) team, dedicated Data Governance (DG) team, or a specific data quality unit, the structure may vary, but the need for visibility remains constant.

Building a comprehensive data quality program by defining its policies, processes, and templates, and selecting and integrating complex tools, is far from an easy job. There is a tremendous amount of work that goes on behind the curtains, often unseen and unappreciated by the broader organization. This is also one of those reasons why many data quality programs lack buy-in and sustained sponsorship. It's high time CDOs and especially DG and DQ teams invest deliberately in showcasing their achievements. It's time they learn to stand out!

As we discussed earlier, your DQ program shouldn't be operating in a silo. It must be inextricably linked to strategic business initiatives. When those business initiatives achieve their KPIs or experience success, it's paramount that the DQ team receives its rightful share of the benefits. Investing in PR and "internal marketing" for this team transforms quiet operational excellence into a powerful beacon that attracts support, fuels collaboration, and solidifies the program's strategic role.

To effectively broadcast real outcomes and give your data quality partners the spotlight, I can suggest these powerful tactics:

Amplify success with executive testimonials

Nothing resonates like hearing a business leader describe, in their own words, how clean data unlocked value in their unit. Executive testimonials provide authentic, high-impact endorsements that resonate throughout the organization.

Think about when you listen to an inspiring podcast. You connect with the speaker's ideas because you see parts of yourself in their story. The same psychology works internally. When a respected business leader openly shares their real experiences, the challenges, the failures, and the wins, it makes your work relatable. It humanizes it. It tells people, "We're in this together, and it's okay to learn and evolve."

Tactics:

- **Video Case Studies:** Film a concise "before-and-after" story. Let the executive outline the challenge, explain how your DQ team's solution worked, and share the tangible results.

- **Podcast or webinar clips:** Host short interviews where C-suite sponsors dive into the business impact of improved data quality. Recordings can live on your intranet, collaboration channels, learning platform, or even on LinkedIn (if policy permits). Hearing firsthand accounts of problem resolution and value creation from peers is incredibly powerful and authentic.

- **Quarterly newsletter features:** Dedicate a page to "Voices of the Business," showcasing quotes and mini-stories from leaders who benefited most.

Host roadshows and in-person events

Face-to-face interactions build trust more quickly than any email or Slack post. We discussed the importance of getting everyone in a room earlier. Small-scale roadshows or town halls create buzz, spark curiosity, and reinforce that a dedicated team is ready to help with data-related challenges. And trust me, it isn't expensive to organize them, and they can also be combined with your other team's collaborative events. These events aren't just for presenting, they're for engaging.

Tactics:

- **Data quality roadshows:** Take your team on the road—host pop-up sessions in different business units. Invite stakeholders from different teams to co-present how DQ improvements directly unlocked value in their area.

Demonstrate demos of new data quality tools or simplified processes. Share quick wins and invite local leaders to speak.

- **"DQ open house" events:** Can be combined with your lunch and learn sessions, for example. Turn a conference room into a mini-expo: poster boards on current initiatives, live demos, feedback on dashboards or processes, open Q&A with DQ teams, etc.

Create a constant buzz

Utilize your organization's digital communication channels to create continuous engagement and buzz around data quality achievements. Reinforcement through digital channels keeps data quality top of mind and invites real-time engagement.

Tactics:

- **Intranet headlines:** Feature a rotating banner or news tile with headlines like "How DQ Drove 5% More Revenue Last Month." Link to deeper articles or videos.

- **Slack/Teams channels:** Maintain a dedicated #data-quality channel where you share daily tips, celebrate wins ("Shout-out Wednesday"), and field quick questions.

- **Interactive polls and mini-quizzes:** Run weekly one-question polls ("Which DQ rule saved us the most time this week?") or 2-question quizzes to reinforce key concepts and engage busy stakeholders.

Translate DQ success into a common language

To ensure your achievements resonate broadly, the content you create must be easily understood by everyone, regardless of their technical or business background. Develop creative ways to explain the complex impacts of data quality.

Tactics:

- **One-page "DQ 101" cheat sheet:** A simple DQ visual glossary (no more than a page) that explains key DQ terms in everyday language, easily searchable in the data catalog, or distributed at roadshows and in onboarding packs.

- **Audience-focused dashboards:** We discussed a lot of this in previous sections. It's essential to visualize the impact and root cause of bad data in a language best understood by the people who are supposed to act on it.

- **Pop-culture analogies:** Explain DQ concepts with references to familiar stories: "Think of missing data as the wayward Jedi—when one goes off course, the whole mission fails." It might not always be helpful, but it's good to create a buzz.

- **Lego-style infographics and bulletins:** Show how data "bricks" fit together, and how missing or misshapen bricks cause the entire structure to wobble.

Go external: Share your story with the world

Presenting at industry events and in external publications not only builds your team's credibility, but also elevates your entire organization's brand as a data-driven leader within your industry domain. Don't limit your success stories to internal audiences. Numerous data and AI conferences take place throughout the year worldwide. Senior executives, in particular, highly value this kind of external visibility and thought leadership, which reinforces their initial sponsorship.

Tactics:

- **Conference talks:** Actively encourage and enable your data quality peers to prepare and share their experiences at external industry conferences or symposiums. Craft short proposals ("How We Recovered $X Million Through Focused DQ Rules"), targeting both data-centric and line-of-business tracks. If you're not from the B2B or software vendor industry, you'll often get free passes to speak at these events.

- **Bylined articles and case studies:** Pitch success stories to industry magazines or online platforms, with clear metrics and human-interest angles.

- **Customer and partner newsletters:** If you work in a B2B context, ask satisfied clients to co-author a testimonial piece on how your clean data improved their experience.

Allocate a dedicated PR and marketing budget

Sustained visibility requires resources. By earmarking even a small percentage of your DG/DQ budget for PR activities like video production, event catering, graphic design, etc., you signal that storytelling and advocacy are as strategic as DQ rule implementation and tool integration.

Tactics:

- **Line-item in annual plan:** Include a "Communications and Engagement" budget for internal events, video shoots, or external sponsorships.

- **Collateral development:** Invest in professional templates for newsletters, slide decks, and infographics to maintain a polished, cohesive look.

- **Cross-team collaboration:** Partner with your corporate communications or marketing department to leverage their expertise and platforms to amplify your message.

I know these tactics might sound like a lot to do, but for data quality (and governance), it's crucial to reinforce their existence and value again and again, until

---

You shift mindsets from seeing DQ as a good-to-have to recognizing it as a must-have.

When you invest in PR by showcasing authentic testimonials, celebrating wins, hosting visible roadshows, and speaking a language everyone understands, you transform your DG/DQ team from an invisible back-office function into a credible and strategic partner.

The more your people see the real, measurable outcomes of good data, the more they trust and champion your work. This visibility attracts new allies, secures stronger sponsorship, and ensures your data quality efforts are woven into the bigger business story, where they necessarily belong!

EIGHT

AI for Data Quality versus Data Quality for AI

Yes, finally, let's jump to AI. No data forum or book can be complete without discussing AI. Over the last few years, Artificial Intelligence, especially Generative AI, has moved from being a buzzword to boardroom agendas to working POCs. From predictive maintenance in manufacturing to customer service chatbots to LLMs that can summarize legal documents or suggest code, AI is everywhere. And with this hype, a fundamental question is often overlooked:

Why are we adopting AI in the first place?

- Is it flattening organizational hierarchies allowing organizations to become more agile?
- To work smarter and more efficiently?
- To save costs and reduce redundancy?
- Because competitors are doing it?

- Or are we just chasing automation for automation's sake?

In my view, at the heart of it, all the rush and these aspirations converge on a single goal: **we want to automate intelligently.** We aim to streamline business processes, generate faster insights, and enable machines to handle repetitive cognitive tasks, allowing humans to focus on what truly matters.

That is the promise of AI: doing things faster, smarter, and cheaper.

Yet as we rush toward AI-driven solutions, a persistent obstacle keeps getting in the way: **poor data quality.** One of the most persistent data quality challenges today stems from our key source systems: both legacy and newly developed cloud-based ERP (Enterprise Resource Planning) applications. Business processes around these systems are often designed directly by business owners in collaboration with IT or dedicated source teams, frequently operating in isolation from the broader data management ecosystem and, crucially, from downstream data consumers. This inherent disconnect between design and ownership is a key reason why data quality issues continue to escalate, albeit silently and significantly.

Adding to this complexity, many of these ERP applications are managed by third-party technology vendors. This creates further dependencies and significant obstacles when internal data teams attempt to trace data lineage, apply critical validations, or resolve inconsistencies. In many cases, cloud ERP reporting solutions provide little to no direct visibility into how reports are generated, and obtaining detailed data lineage insights can take weeks (if they are available at all). In many cases, this acts as a hidden yet significant cost to organizations, often running into millions of dollars annually.

Worse still, there's an assumption that AI teams, data teams (or consultants), and source data teams will naturally collaborate. In reality, source data teams are swamped by operational priorities and technical debt, while AI teams pursue new models and insights, and internal data teams struggle to get everyone on the same page for policies, processes, and technology. This misalignment creates delays, undermines trust, and jeopardizes the very AI initiatives we hope will accelerate our business.

That's why our focus must be on sustained, **step-by-step automation** that bridges these gaps, basically using AI not just as a flashy endpoint but as an enabler of clearer communication, tighter engagement, and stronger data quality foundations.

And this brings us to two very different but equally important perspectives:

Data quality for AI

No matter how advanced the model is, AI cannot alone overcome poor data. Whether you're using large language models, predictive engines, or any other AI-powered tool, the principle of "garbage in, garbage out" still applies. These systems are essentially sophisticated data-transformation pipelines: any inaccuracies, gaps, or inconsistencies in your input will be magnified in the output. What makes this especially dangerous is that AI often sounds authoritative and polished, making errors more challenging to spot.

I've experienced this firsthand: on several occasions, I've posed simple business questions to an LLM and received confident, well-phrased answers that were completely incorrect. They read like presentation-ready insights, until I paused to fact-check. That unsettling "Wait—what?" moment is a reminder that we must never accept AI outputs at face value without rigorous validation.

Another common pattern is that most organizational AI efforts focus on internal processes like chatbots, copilots, and automated reports, rather than customer-facing applications. The reason is largely regulatory. As soon as you expose AI externally, stringent data regulations and AI-specific laws come into play. Companies must then demonstrate documented data capabilities such as lineage information, quality metrics, metadata standards, and data security policies for every response the AI generates. Many organizations lack those foundations and can't answer basic questions about how a model arrived at its conclusions. Only a few have successfully built the necessary data governance frameworks to navigate these requirements on a scale.

> *You can't blindly trust even the smartest AI without validating the data behind it.*

Always treat AI responses as hypotheses to be tested, not as guaranteed truths.

Hence, it's very critical to consider the points below:

- **Blind trust is dangerous:** We all work mostly in fast-paced, tight-scheduled work environments, and it's alarmingly easy to accept an LLM's output at face value, especially when a deadline looms. However, one wrong figure in a financial forecast, an incorrect assumption in market research, or a subtly biased recommendation can derail entire projects, leading to significant financial losses or reputational damage. Hence, it's critical to always reserve time for fact-checking critical AI-generated responses.

- **Garbage In, Garbage Out at all levels:** I know this phrase might be a bit overhyped, but its underlying premise still stands true. And it's applicable not only to your data(sets), but also to its metadata. If your metadata, knowledge graphs, or lineage information used to prepare your data are incomplete, inaccurate, or biased, the model will inevitably reflect those flaws, producing outputs that are equally, if not more, flawed. AI amplifies the quality of its inputs, whether good or bad.

- **Quality gates at every stage:** Just as you enforce rigorous data validation checks in your traditional ETL (Extract, Transform, Load) processes, you need to establish robust "quality gates" around your AI workflows.

    o **Input gates:** These checks verify the cleanliness, completeness, accuracy, and relevance of your source data (and metadata) *before* it ever reaches the AI model. They act as the first line of defense, ensuring your model is trained or fed only with trustworthy information.

    o **Output gates:** These apply business rules, human review, or automated anomaly detection to flag inconsistencies, illogical outputs, or potentially biased content generated by the AI. They are the final safeguard against AI-generated content influencing business decisions or customer interactions.

- **End-to-end data management is the foundation:** A successful AI strategy is impossible without a strong data foundation. The quality of your data inputs, the integrity of your transformation logic, and the reliability of your final AI outputs all depend on robust data management practices, including meticulous metadata management, clear data lineage tracking, stringent access controls, and continuous data quality monitoring. These elements collectively form the foundation upon which reliable AI is built.

- **Build once, trust always:** Effective data governance is the key pillar revolving around all the points mentioned above. Investing in comprehensive data governance (and data quality) management frameworks up front pays dividends as AI initiatives scale. When your data assets are consistently governed, documented, and monitored, each new model can be launched with confidence, eliminating the need to repeat foundational work.

So, before you hit "Generate" or deploy that next AI model, ask yourself these critical questions:

- Have I thoroughly verified the inputs going into my model?
- Am I adequately prepared to catch unexpected errors or biases in the output?
- How tightly integrated are my data quality processes with my AI development and operational workflows?

While we are all speeding toward AI-driven decision-making and automation, getting the basics right is more important than ever. Always start with a rock-solid data foundation, and only then let your AI build transformative capabilities on top of that.

AI for data quality

Now let's flip the lens.

> *While data quality is foundational to trustworthy AI, the reverse is also true: AI can play a powerful role in enhancing data quality, making it better, faster, and more scalable.*

Many data governance and quality software vendors today are jumping on the AI bandwagon by labeling as AI what's essentially simple data quality rule automation or process improvement suggestions. Tasks that should've been solved ten years ago are being resold today as "AI-driven" just because there's a model in the background.

That's not what I mean when I say "AI for data quality."

True AI for DQ should be:

- **User-centric:** Tailored to the people who build, consume, and govern data.
- **Problem-specific:** Designed to address concrete pain points rather than generic automation.
- **Value-oriented:** Measured by improvements in data trust, onboarding speed, and downstream business impact.

When applied thoughtfully and targeted towards the real needs of data professionals and business users, AI can bring genuine breakthroughs to data quality management.

Below are some practical applications where AI truly helps in data quality:

Intelligent rule suggestions

Traditional DQ tooling often relies on users manually defining rules or choosing from generic, template-driven options. AI introduces a transformative leap in this space.

Instead of suggesting a rule based purely on column names or basic data types, AI can learn from historical usage patterns, issue logs, metadata, lineage graphs, and prior remediation activities. By doing so, it can proactively recommend more relevant and context-sensitive data quality rules, tailored not only to the dataset in question but also to its specific usage history and quality trends.

For data stewards and analysts, this significantly reduces the friction of rule creation, accelerates implementation, and ensures higher rule relevance across domains.

Smart profiling and anomaly detection

Data profiling is foundational to understanding the health and usability of data. However, traditional profiling methods, which focus on min/max, null counts, value ranges, and distributions, are often insufficient to build a comprehensive understanding of data quality.

AI can go several steps further. By continuously analyzing patterns and shifts over time, AI systems can detect subtle anomalies, correlations, statistical drifts, and outliers that are often missed by standard rules. It can also evaluate datasets for their "fitness for use" against defined business objectives or quality thresholds.

This enables proactive detection of emerging issues and more accurate assessments of which datasets are suitable or unsuitable for a particular use case. For organizations aiming to scale data use across teams, this is an invaluable capability.

Automated data lineage and relationship discovery

Understanding data lineage, including how data moves and transforms across systems, is critical for root cause analysis, impact assessments, and overall trust in data. But capturing lineage, especially at the column level and across diverse platforms, remains a significant challenge for even the most advanced organizations. Even the best-of-breed data governance tools do not support end-to-end lineage capability.

AI can dramatically reduce the burden of lineage mapping. By using techniques such as vector embeddings, pattern recognition, and graph traversal, AI can automatically parse SQL code, system logs, pipeline metadata, and data flow diagrams to reconstruct lineage paths. This enables the creation of near-real-time lineage maps that are far more complete and dynamic than those built manually.

AI can also detect relationships across disparate datasets, uncovering undocumented dependencies and hidden links that matter deeply when diagnosing DQ issues or planning schema changes.

"Governance as Code" with AI assistance

I bet you've heard of the term 'federated computational governance.' It's a pillar of modern data mesh and data product strategies, promoting the codification of policies and their application programmatically, which we can also refer to as "governance as code."

This approach ensures that data products, datasets, and pipelines comply with predefined rules (e.g., naming conventions, SLOs, privacy thresholds) *before* they are published or consumed. A big part of data contract enforcement relies on the governance as code concept.

AI can assist this complex process by:

- Generating policy templates based on existing usage patterns.
- Validating incoming data assets against predefined governance rules.

- Flagging violations or compliance gaps early in the lifecycle.
- Assisting with data contract creation by interpreting schema changes, inferring intent, and aligning them with SLOs.

This drastically reduces the need for manual enforcement, shortens review cycles, and enables more scalable and federated governance.

AI-powered remediation recommendations

Detecting data quality issues is only half the battle; the more challenging part is fixing them. AI can guide this process. We previously discussed how data teams assist the source system personnel with root-cause identification. I believe AI can play a significant role in that.

AI can provide intelligent remediation by analyzing the nature of data defects and suggesting corrective actions.

For example, if city names in a dataset are inconsistently formatted or misspelled, AI models can reference external master datasets or historical corrections to propose the most likely intended values. It can recommend batch-cleaning scripts, validate potential fixes through similar scores or confidence levels, and even prioritize issues by projected business impact.

This can be particularly useful in large, heterogeneous data environments where manual triage is infeasible.

Natural Language Processing (NLP) for rule extraction

Many critical business rules are hidden in documents such as policy manuals, Excel spreadsheets, emails, or Confluence pages. These "soft rules" often fail to be incorporated into data systems, resulting in blind spots or misaligned expectations.

AI, particularly through natural language processing (NLP), can be utilized to extract relevant rules, thresholds, and definitions from these documents. Once extracted, these can be converted into actionable DQ checks or documented as part of metadata. This ensures that no critical business logic gets lost or overlooked during implementation.

Co-pilot experiences for DQ interactions

The rise of LLM-powered co-pilot experiences has opened conversational interfaces for querying and managing data. However, the effectiveness of these assistants depends entirely on the underlying metadata, DQ definitions, lineage information, and business glossary.

Where this metadata is complete and accurate, AI-powered co-pilots can serve as intelligent assistants, enabling users to query data health, explain rule failures, suggest fixes, or even simulate the impact of proposed changes. Without that metadata foundation, however, such responses remain vague and unhelpful.

This reinforces the need for AI and metadata management to be deeply integrated.

Metadata/catalog sync

Finally, AI can help with a task that remains a persistent operational burden: synchronizing DQ metrics and profiling results back into your data catalog or metadata layer.

By automatically tagging datasets with quality scores, issue history, lineage context, and usage metadata, AI can enrich your data catalog or data marketplace experience for both business and technical users. It provides a single pane of glass for data discovery and quality monitoring, enabling users to make informed decisions about data usage.

Automating this metadata feedback loop, often an afterthought in many programs, can drive far greater transparency, usability, and trust in your data ecosystem.

Unstructured data quality analysis

As AI initiatives grow in complexity and ambition, there is an increasing reliance on unstructured data, spanning across PDFs, scanned documents, emails, GitHub repositories, SharePoint files,

Slack channels, and Confluence pages. These often contain valuable context, business logic, or reference material that AI models depend upon. Many experts have rightly flagged the challenges of assessing quality in these formats, given their inconsistent structure, ambiguous context, and fragmented storage.

Yet, despite the format, I believe the fundamentals of data quality still apply.

You still need to define clear quality criteria (think of your DQ dimensions), even if you're working with text, scanned images, or handwritten notes. You still need 'someone' to act on it, and you will still need to translate the impact into a language everyone understands.

Many companies and software vendors are in advanced stages of evaluating how AI can assist in extracting metadata, automatically tagging content by category or topic, identifying gaps or inconsistencies in the information, and linking content to structured datasets for improved understanding. In more mature implementations, AI can prioritize issues based on inferred usage patterns, flag non-compliance with regulatory or policy-based standards, and even suggest remediation steps such as rewriting ambiguous content, linking to canonical sources, or assigning ownership.

The goal remains the same: to bring visibility, structure, and trust to data, even if it starts its life as an unstructured asset.

Remember, AI for data quality is not about replacing human judgment; it's about amplifying it!

Data quality for AI and ***AI for data quality*** *are not interchangeable but rather mutually reinforcing.*

High-quality, governed data is the only reliable fuel for AI engines. Conversely, AI techniques, applied thoughtfully, can elevate data-quality processes to new levels of scale, speed, and precision.

Can gamification drive data quality engagement?

You might be curious after reading the engagement tactics and wonder - How about gamifying the DQ experience? Can AI help us with that?

Many data teams have experimented with AI-enabled leaderboards, point systems, and badges, aiming to drive curiosity, engagement, and ownership among internal users who regularly interact with data.

While gamification can be tempting to inject fun into data tasks, I believe it only helps to a certain extent. For senior executives, while it might create some initial buzz, it rarely drives true, sustained engagement. Remember, we are talking about busy leaders whose time is precious.

In my field of data management, where there's an overwhelming amount of noise, especially around AI and automation, the advice to **"Keep it Simple"** feels incredibly relevant. Everyone seems to be chasing complexity: advanced solutions, cutting-edge tools, and the latest buzzwords. But I've always believed in the importance of starting with the basics.

Simple questions like:

- Do we even know where our data is coming from?
- What does 'good' quality data mean for *you*, specifically?
- Have we set up the right foundation before chasing "intelligent AI" solutions?

> *I've learned that you don't need to overcomplicate things to make an impact.*

Sometimes, the best rewards are the simplest ones: **automation and simplification**. True engagement is driven by seeing direct business impact. When a data steward notices that a single automated rule prevented a costly error, that serves as a far more compelling motivator than earning a digital badge. Focusing on these small outcomes can save significant time for your people and garner far greater appreciation from all stakeholders.

Consider these automation-driven incentives as practical alternatives to gamification:

- **Instant expert finder:** A simple catalog interface that, with one search, shows you exactly who owns which data asset, who built the last dashboard, or who resolved the most recent quality issue. No badges, just fast answers!

- **Seamless knowledge sharing:** Creating an easy and collaborative way to share learnings and experiences about data quality or data in general across teams. This could involve an AI-powered search for past solutions or the creation of automated summaries of common issues.

- **One-click DQ workflows:** Enable domain users to trigger data quality rules, remediation scripts, or data refreshes with a single button in the data marketplace or DQ tool, eliminating complex ticket creation process queues and lengthy change requests.

- **DQ results at point of consumption:** As discussed earlier, bringing DQ insights directly to where users are consuming data (e.g., dashboards, collaboration tools).

- **Simplified data access:** Allowing users to request and gain access to data in just a few streamlined steps, rather than navigating complex bureaucratic processes.

- **Translation into simple language:** Utilizing AI to translate complex DQ findings into plain, understandable business language. (As I couldn't emphasize this point enough earlier, it's fundamental.)

- Ensuring effortless, self-service access to data definitions and metadata.

- Deploying data quality workflows with a simple click.

- Allowing users to request and gain access to data in just a few streamlined steps.

I'm not saying you shouldn't have a touch of fun when it comes to communicating data quality. It indeed ignites a positive outlook towards data quality.

While games can help bond and communicate during in-person engagement, for online interaction, it's paramount to focus on clear communication and efficiency. I still value in-person workshops and fun events far more than purely online games for helping establish trust and collaboration within and across teams, and for demonstrating how data quality can truly make their jobs easier and more rewarding.

Ultimately, the best incentive is often to make the "right" thing (good data quality) the "easy" thing.

NINE

Which is the right tool
for our data quality program?

I had to talk about this critical question. Every boardroom conversation eventually turns to tools. I've lost track of how many times CDOs and data leaders have leaned forward in a meeting and asked: "We've already spent half a million on data quality and governance platforms, why aren't we data-driven yet?" Their VPs are still raising the same questions:

- "Why is my data still unclean?"
- "Why do our reporting SLAs keep slipping?"
- "Why are business owners drowning in hundreds of alerts every Monday?"
- "Why does our DQ dashboard miss the metrics leadership actually cares about?"
- "Why do simple data questions become multi-week projects?"

- "Why is it taking so long to build a simple forecasting report?"

The truth is, **tools alone were never the core problem**.

The market is flooded with vendors, and almost every industry conference sees numerous providers attempting to lure data and business executives, promising that their tool or software will magically solve all their data quality challenges. Some experts will enthusiastically recommend "Tool X" because it worked wonders for them in a different context. Others will emphatically mention that same "Tool X" is terrible because it's too technical. Some might opt for open source "Tool Y," while others will follow research reports blindly and choose "Tool Z" because it's been labeled a "leader" in some quadrant. Based on my own experience in this field,

---

Around 60% of data governance and data quality initiatives fail precisely because organizations choose tools first, without understanding their own people, processes, and priorities.

Why tools come second

Data quality is fundamentally about understanding and solving your organization's unique challenges, not about deploying the fanciest stack; it's about deeply understanding your organization's specific data struggles and human behaviors. Think of tools as the solution to a problem, not the starting point for finding problems.

If you don't first have a clear understanding of your data's complete journey, who works with it, what challenges they face, and why good data matters to them, how can any tool magically fix your problems?

I've had my share of hands-on experiences with leading tools across various organizations. While there's no single, exhaustive formula for tool selection, below is my take on a more effective process, prioritizing understanding and context over feature lists.

Strategic approach to tool selection

1. **Start with the basics: People and process first.** Before investing in any tool, ensure that your data governance (and quality) basics are firmly in order. Remember, effective governance is primarily about people and processes, not just technology. Laying this groundwork, such as defining what 'good' data means to us, formalizing clear roles, establishing communication channels, etc., is the essential first step.

2. **Ownership and accountability: Know who's driving.** Does your organization already have a clear data ownership structure in place? Are business stakeholders

prepared to embrace new governance processes? Is there a centralized data governance and data quality team, or a core function, to lead and collaborate on all data quality requests? If you have these foundational elements, you're on the right track to move forward successfully with a tool.

3. **Comprehensive assessment: Understand your unique ecosystem.** The foundation of sound tool selection lies in a detailed assessment of your unique organizational context. This involves asking crucial questions that inform your tool strategy:

   o **Data journey visibility:** Do you track your data's complete journey? Do you know where your data comes from, who changed it, and if alerts tell you what's wrong before it becomes a disaster?

   o **Scalability:** What systems, platforms, tools, or home-grown solutions are already in place? What are your infrastructure limitations? Not every team needs an enterprise platform; some may be effective with code-based validations, Confluence trackers, or lightweight solutions.

   o **User landscape:** Which roles interact with data daily—analysts, stewards, engineers? What specific challenges do they face? What kind of users will primarily manage data quality activities?

4. **Use-case clarity: Define the problem before the solution.** The direct outcome of your comprehensive assessment should be a set of clearly pinpointed use cases for the tool. Data quality shouldn't be a siloed program. These cases must be thoroughly discussed and agreed upon with the very people who will be using the platform. The selection criteria should prioritize tools that help you take a preventive approach rather than merely a reactive one in your data quality efforts.

5. **Embrace a multi-tool reality.** One tool seldom fits all your data governance and quality needs.

There is no single tool currently available on the market that does it 'all' perfectly across the entire data quality spectrum.

Therefore, be prepared for a multi-tool approach. Consider conducting Minimum Viable Product (MVP) pilots or Proof of Concept (POC) tests to validate your critical use cases before committing to a full platform rollout. Measure outcomes with tangible results in mind, such as reduction in errors, time saved, and SLA improvements. These "proof points" beat any vendor checklist.

Alternatively, explore ways to maximize the value of your existing technology stack. Many cloud vendors, like Microsoft or AWS, now offer comprehensive data governance solutions with built-in data quality modules. While still evolving, these integrated platforms can effectively tackle many of your use cases, especially if you're already using their cloud ecosystem.

6. **Technical versus business focused: Understand the nuance.** As we've discussed earlier in this book, there's a fundamental difference between technical data quality and business data quality. Many tools on the market, especially those led by modern data platforms, are primarily focused on technical pipeline-related checks, often confined to data that moves through or is engineered within that specific data platform.

There is also a completely different category of data observability tooling. We discussed at length what data observability is supposed to do. Not all standard DQ tools will cover observability, and vice versa. Ensure you're crystal clear about whether your primary need is for technical pipeline validation, business rule enforcement, data observability, or a combination of these.

7. **Tools are only as good as their users: Enablement is key.** No doubt, some great tools on the market promise to make your life easier. But they are only effective if your stakeholders use them. A tool is not a magic wand; it requires dedicated time, a commitment to adoption, proper training, and the consistent application of best

practices across the platform. Without this user enablement, even the most advanced tool becomes expensive shelfware gathering digital dust.

I'm not going to argue on **Build versus Buy**. Many successful organizations have built effective in-house solutions tailored to their unique data quality needs, and they've made it work. But this path demands deep technical expertise, patience, ongoing investment, and a strong culture of ownership. Adoption can be slow, especially when DIY tools lack the polish and usability of commercial platforms.

Ultimately, selecting the right data quality tool isn't a quick win or a checklist exercise. It's a strategic decision rooted in your business priorities, team dynamics, and long-term goals. Don't chase the tool with the most features; choose the one that fits your organization's maturity, infrastructure, culture, and real-world challenges.

The DQ tool selection process is more about the fit than the features!

Heartfelt Note to all DQ Practitioners

"**Are we doing enough? Does anyone even care about what we do?**"

A young data quality analyst asked me this not long ago. It caught me off guard, not because I hadn't thought about it, but because I had asked myself the same question many years ago, early on my journey.

The truth is, working in data governance or data quality doesn't always come with a spotlight. It rarely makes headlines, and it often struggles to draw attention in boardrooms where revenue, growth, and innovation dominate the conversation. Our work is foundational, but its impact isn't always immediate or appreciated.

Yes, the journey can sometimes feel solitary. I've faced countless situations where DQ was brushed aside with comments like, "*This isn't our priority right now,*" or "*Let's park it for the next quarter.*"

However, times are changing. Thanks to the rapid adoption of Generative AI, many organizations have been compelled to re-evaluate their stance on data quality. In fact, data quality, which was once a niche topic, is now a highlight discussion across virtually all major industry conferences, customer conversations, and community events this year. Organizations are finally waking up to the reality that there is no AI without trusted data.

I've learned along the way that good data silently powers great decisions.

And more than ever, it's becoming the backbone of every function, every team, and every AI initiative in modern organizations. It's not loud, but it's essential. This is our moment in the sun.

In my view, over the next five years, most people will begin their workday not with emails, but with a dashboard—a clean, intuitive interface that displays exactly the data they need for their work, how it's performing, and what they need to act on. We're not far from that reality.

What makes a good data quality practitioner?

I am often asked on platforms like LinkedIn: "How can we become good DQ practitioners?"

Yes, there's plenty of content out there: frameworks, books, certifications, templates. They certainly help. But what matters? In my view, it's about **understanding the core.** Not just memorizing methods but internalizing the "why" behind them. Knowing enough to re-derive any concept on the spot and being able to explain it in plain language. **That's what makes you good at this.**

And please, don't try to retrofit every framework you find into your organization. Your data quality setup is *yours.* It's *unique.* Keep it simple. Stick to basics. Let it grow with your people.

But before I close, I want to leave you with one heartfelt message, one that's shaped my journey, and I hope stays with you too:

It's okay to be vulnerable.

In our field, that might sound counterintuitive. We're expected to know the answers, resolve issues, and drive compliance. But vulnerability is not weakness; it's a quiet strength.

Some of the most powerful breakthroughs come not from showcasing expertise, but from admitting I didn't have all the answers. Whether it was during team retros, coffee chats with business leaders, or late-night problem-solving with peers, being honest created space for real dialogue and deeper trust. I always raised my hands to solve the data problems faced by businesses. I failed more than I succeeded, but I never stopped showing up. And that, more than anything, has shaped my growth.

So ask for help. Share what you're struggling with. Tell your leaders *why* DQ matters, not just *what* it is. Because once they understand your intent, they'll start to value your work in a whole new light.

In conclusion, to every data quality practitioner reading this: **Keep the boat sailing**. Our work is more than dashboards, frameworks, and rules. It's about creating trust, enabling insight, and building a culture where data is treated not as an afterthought, but as an asset. In a world obsessed with instant gratification, it's easy to forget that some of the most important things take time to build, and data trust is one of them.

Let's continue to support one another, to share openly, and to build a community where DQ professionals feel seen, heard, and empowered. Because the work we are doing is quietly shaping the future of our organization, even if not everyone realizes it just yet.

Thank you for everything you do.

Thank you for reading this book.

Thank you for believing in me and this mission.

Keep going. We're just getting started!

Index